3

AVENUES

English Grammar

Lynne Gaetz

PEARSON

Montréal

Managing Editor
Sharnee Chait

Editor
Lucie Turcotte

Copy Editor
Stacey Berman

Proofreader
Katie Moore

Coordination, Rights and Permissions
Pierre Richard Bernier

Art Director
Hélène Cousineau

Graphic Design Coordinator
Lyse LeBlanc

Book Design and Layout
Interscript

Cover Design
Frédérique Bouvier

Cover Artwork
Pietro Adamo, *Citta Series*, 2009. Mixed media on paper, 36 x 24 inches. Courtesy of Progressive Fine Art and Galerie Beauchamp.
ERPI publishes and distributes PEARSON ELT products in Canada.

1611 Crémazie Boulevard East, 10th Floor
Montréal, Québec H2M 2P2
Canada
Telephone: 1 800 263-3678
Fax: 514 334-4720
information@pearsonerpi.com
pearsonerpi.com

Registration of copyright – Bibliothèque et Archives nationales du Québec, 2013
Registration of copyright – Library and Archives Canada, 2013

Printed in Canada 456789 II 17 16 15
ISBN 978-2-7613-5122-5 135122 ABCD ENV94

Acknowledgements

Many people helped produce what you hold in your hands. I would like to express sincere thanks to

- Sharnee Chait for her valuable expertise;
- Lucie Turcotte for her patience and insight while editing this book;
- Julie Hough for her enthusiasm, which helped ignite this project;
- My students at Collège Lionel-Groulx for their insightful feedback;
- Diego Pelaez for his valuable contributions to this manuscript and My eLab;
- Interscript for the creative layout.

Finally, I dedicate this to my children Diego and Rebeka.

This book is printed on paper made in Québec from 100% post-consumer recycled materials, processed chlorine-free, certified Eco-Logo, and manufactured using biogas energy.

TABLE OF CONTENTS

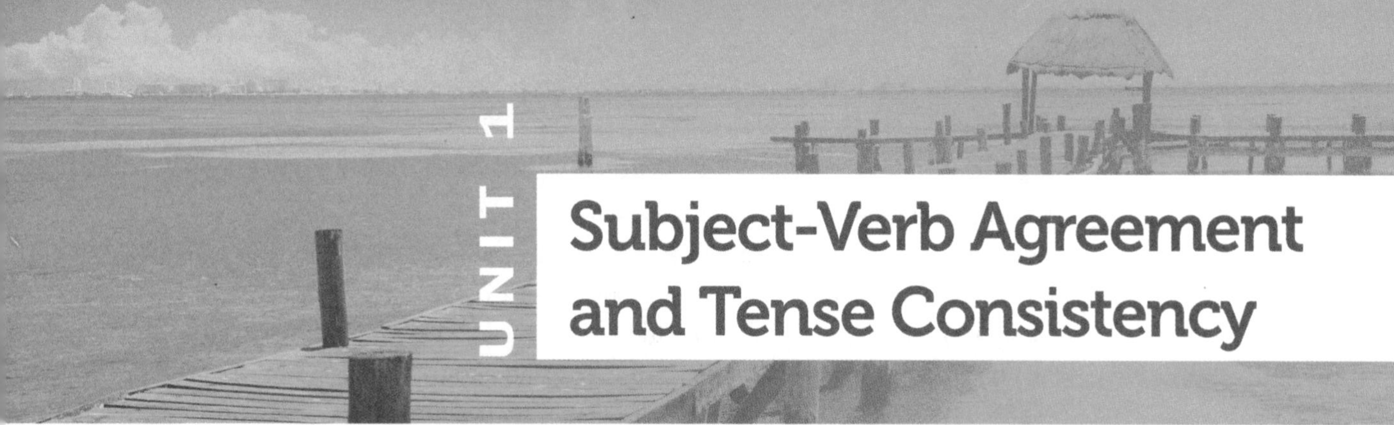

UNIT 1 Subject-Verb Agreement and Tense Consistency

Preview

FIND THE DIFFERENCES

What are six differences between these photos? On a separate sheet of paper, write complete sentences about six differences.

EXAMPLE: In B, there are birds in the sky.

A.

B.

Subject-Verb Agreement: Forms and Usage

PRESENT TENSE AGREEMENT

There are two forms of present tense verbs: the base form and the third-person-singular form. Use the base form when the subject is *I*, *you*, *we*, or *they*.

Lifeguards **take** special courses. I **know** two lifeguards. We **discuss** life-saving techniques.

Add –*s* or –*es* to verbs that follow *he*, *she*, or *it*. In other words, if the subject is one person, place, or thing, but not *you* or *I*, the verb must take an –s or –es ending.

One person: The doctor **treats** many patients.
One place: The clinic **closes** on Sundays.
One thing: The file **contains** personal information.

TIP

Spelling Rules for the Third-Person Singular Form

Add *–es* to verbs ending in *–s*, *–sh*, *–ss*, *–ch*, *–o*, or *–x*.

teach ▶ teach**es** do ▶ do**es**

When a verb ends in a consonant + *–y*, change *–y* to *–ies*.

carry ▶ carr**ies** study ▶ stud**ies**

When a verb ends in a vowel + *–y*, keep the *–y* and add *–s*.

say ▶ say**s** destroy ▶ destroy**s**

PAST TENSE AGREEMENT

Almost all verbs have only one past tense form, so you don't have to modify it when the subject changes. The only verb that requires specific subject-verb agreement in its past tense form is the verb *be*, which has two past forms: *was* and *were*.

I / He / She / It **was** in the living room.
You / We / They **were** in the kitchen.

THERE + BE

When a sentence begins with *There*, the real subject follows the verb *be*.

There **is / was** + one thing: There **was** a fire on Elm Street.
There **are / were** + two or more things: There **were** many firefighters at the site.

SPECIAL SUBJECTS

Gerunds

Sometimes a gerund (*–ing* form of the verb) is the singular subject of a sentence.

Snowboarding requires good reflexes.

Indefinite Pronouns

Indefinite pronouns beginning with *every*, *some*, *any*, or *no* are considered singular. To help remember this rule, notice that the last part of each word is a singular subject.

everybody	everyone	everything	everywhere
somebody	someone	something	somewhere
anybody	anyone	anything	anywhere
nobody	no one	nothing	nowhere

Everyone **has** fears, but nobody **likes** to admit it.

Each* and *Every

If you put one or more singular nouns (joined by *and*) after *each* and *every*, the verb remains singular.

Every firefighter **wears** safety gear. Each man and woman **works** hard.

Agreement with Collective Nouns

Collective nouns refer to groups of people or things. Here are some common collective nouns:

army	class	crowd	group	public
association	club	family	jury	organization
audience	committee	gang	mob	society
band	company	government	population	team

Generally, a group acts as a unit, so you must use it with the singular form of the verb.

The jury **is** ready to read the verdict.

If the members of the group act individually, use the plural form of the verb. It is a good idea to reword the sentence using a phrase such as *members of*.

Acceptable: The jury **are** not able to come to an agreement.
Better: The members of the jury **are** not able to come to an agreement.

Practice

EXERCISE 1 **SUBJECT-VERB AGREEMENT**

Underline and correct ten errors in subject-verb agreement. If you make mistakes, review the rules about special subjects on the previous page.

travels
EXAMPLE: Mark McCrum travel around the world.

1. Every man and woman share similar expressions, along with an understanding of their underlying meaning. That's why everybody react badly to a frown. But gestures and traditions is not the same all over the world. In his book *Going Dutch in Beijing*, Mark McCrum warn his readers about some cultural faux pas.

2. Many of McCrum's examples is humorous. For example, in Japan, if someone blow his nose in public, others will be disgusted. Nobody like to see that. And holding hands are not a sign of romance in many cultures. In Saudi Arabia, for example, a man will grasp another man's hand as a sign of respect. However, when a man and woman holds hands, it is not culturally acceptable. In South Africa, everyone do a three-part handshake. People should be careful about their gestures when they are abroad.

TIP

Police Is Considered Plural

Many nouns that refer to a group, such as *association*, are collective and are considered singular. *Police* is also a collective noun, but it is thought of as plural because the word *officers* is implied but not stated.

The police **have** a protester in custody.

EXERCISE 2 **AGREEMENT IN PRESENT AND PAST TENSES**

Underline the appropriate verbs in parentheses. Be especially careful with collective nouns.

EXAMPLE: The committee (have / <u>has</u>) five members.

1. Kate is part of a survival club that (have / has) many meetings. Kate's group (meet / meets) once a month. Sometimes, the police (visit / visits) the club to tell the group how to survive in certain scenarios. For example, yesterday, an officer (was / were) a guest. Officer Wells discussed what to do if someone (fall / falls) through the ice. She explained that the body (lose / loses) heat twenty-five times faster in water than in air. Hypothermia (is / are) a likely result of falling through the ice into the lake below.

2. Last year, at our local lake, there (was / were) forty accidents in which people fell through the ice. Many members of the public (was / were) not careful. Some outdoor enthusiasts (was / were) reckless when they took snowmobiles onto the thin ice. Police (was / were) called in many of the cases. Luckily, there (was / were) no fatalities last winter. My family (live / lives) near a lake, and so do many others. These families should learn some survival techniques.

3. At the club, Officer Wells also discussed what to do if a rattlesnake (bite / bites) someone. There (is / are) a common myth that people should suck out the poison. However, (do / does) not suck out the poison! When Wells speaks, the audience always (listen / listens) carefully.

MORE THAN ONE SUBJECT

There are special agreement rules when a sentence contains more than one subject.

And*, *Or*, and *Nor

When two or more subjects are joined by *and*, use the plural form of the verb. However, when subjects are joined by *or* or *nor*, match the verb with the subject closest to it.

→

plural

Neither Anna **nor** her children **watch** television.

singular

Either the children **or** Clara **is** allergic to dust.

As Well As* and *Along With

The interrupting expressions *as well as* and *along with* don't follow the same rules as *and*. They do not form compound subjects. The real subject is before the interrupting expression.

Flora, Jamal, **and** Kaitlin **work** as firefighters.
Flora, **as well as** Jamal and Kaitlin, **works** as a firefighter.

TIP

Two-Verb Constructions

Sometimes two verbs are separated by a noun or pronoun. Examples are "**make** it **work**" or "**help** him **finish**." Look at the following example. Notice that you must use the base form of the second verb.

base form / base form

Milk **makes** Jess **feel** sick. Sometimes he **helps** me **cook**.

EXERCISE 3 **CORRECTING AGREEMENT ERRORS**

Underline and correct ten errors in subject-verb agreement.

are

EXAMPLE: There is some interesting stories of survival against the odds.

1. One survival story makes everyone feels worried. Do a GPS device help or harms drivers? In 2011, Rita Chretien, as well as her husband, Albert, were in Nevada. They had left their home in Penticton, BC, and they were going to Las Vegas. Looking for a shortcut, they was dependent on their GPS. The device led them off-track and into the remote wilderness. According to Chretien, there was no houses in the vicinity.

2. Albert Chretien decided to look for help. For more than forty days, Rita was alone. Neither her husband nor any rescue team were nearby. Candy, as well as some fish-oil pills, were all that Rita had

→

to eat. Finally, on the forty-ninth day, Rita's luck changed. Chad Herman, along with two of his friends, were looking for antlers. The trio found the very sick Rita, but they never found her husband. Today, Chretien's faith helps her survives the loss of her husband.

INTERRUPTING WORDS AND PHRASES

Words that are between the subject and the verb can cause confusion about subject-verb agreement. In such cases, look for the subject and then make sure that the verb agrees with it.

Some books [that I read in my first college course] **are** about nature.

Agreement After Prepositional Phrases

A prepositional phrase is made up of a preposition and its object (a noun or a pronoun). The object of the prepositional phrase is *not* the subject of the sentence. In the following sentence, the subject and verb are "interrupted" by a prepositional phrase.

The man [with the tattoos] **has** red hair.

Be particularly careful with phrases containing *of the*. In the next examples, the subject appears before *of the*.

One **of the** most annoying neighbours in our district **knows** everybody's secrets.
A photo **of the** cars **appears** in the magazine.
Each **of the** photos **is** in colour.

Exception: Expressions of quantity don't follow the preceding *of the* rule. When the subject is an expression of quantity—*the majority of*, *one third of*, *a part of*, *10 percent of*, *the rest of*—the verb agrees with the noun that follows *of* (*the*).

The majority **of the** audience **likes** the show.
About 20 percent **of the** viewers **watch** the program each week.

EXERCISE 4 CORRECTING AGREEMENT ERRORS

In the following passage, twelve verbs are underlined. Of these, correct the eight verb errors and write *C* over the four correct verbs.

encounter
EXAMPLE: About 5 percent of the airline industry's passengers encounters problems during flights.

1. An earthquake, as well as a volcanic eruption or tsunami, are unpredictable. Although some disasters claim no lives, the majority is deadly. After a tragedy, one of the most common reactions are to panic. According to Dr. Leach, author of *Survivor Psychology*, 95 percent of the population panics within the first three

hours of living through a disaster. The majority of victims doesn't know how to react. Only 5 percent of people remains calm and clear-headed. Even if somebody survive the physical trauma, he or she may not necessarily survive the psychological trauma.

2. Ultimately, what do specialists know about survival? The majority believes that good physical and psychological health help people get through a crisis. Maybe everybody have the ability to survive.

INTERRUPTING WORDS: *WHO*, *WHICH*, AND *THAT*

Some sentences include a relative clause beginning with the pronouns *who*, *which*, or *that*. In the relative clause, the verb must agree with the antecedent of *who*, *which*, or *that*.

> She is a writer **who lives** in Jamaica.
> Here are some stories **that explore** unsolved mysteries.
> One book, **which appears** online, **discusses** a secret island.

EXERCISE 5 **AGREEMENT AFTER INTERRUPTING WORDS**

The next adapted excerpt is from the H. G. Wells novel *The Island of Doctor Moreau*. Read the text. Circle the subject of each verb in parentheses and then underline the correct verb form.

EXAMPLE: There is something in the starlight that (loosen / loosens) one's tongue.

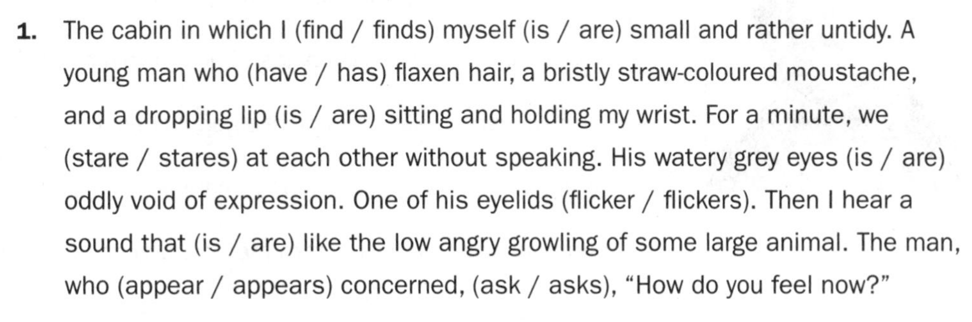

1. The cabin in which I (find / finds) myself (is / are) small and rather untidy. A young man who (have / has) flaxen hair, a bristly straw-coloured moustache, and a dropping lip (is / are) sitting and holding my wrist. For a minute, we (stare / stares) at each other without speaking. His watery grey eyes (is / are) oddly void of expression. One of his eyelids (flicker / flickers). Then I hear a sound that (is / are) like the low angry growling of some large animal. The man, who (appear / appears) concerned, (ask / asks), "How do you feel now?"

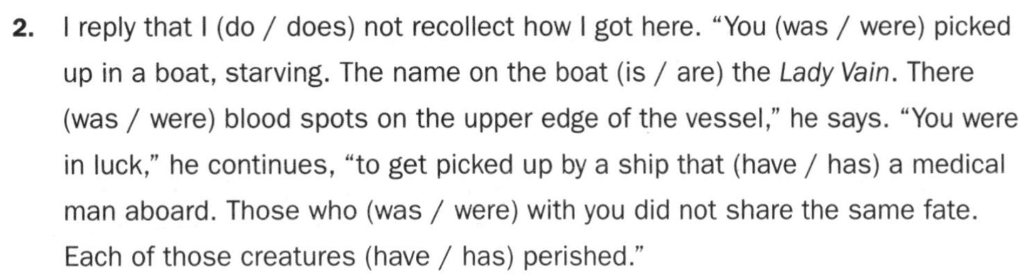

2. I reply that I (do / does) not recollect how I got here. "You (was / were) picked up in a boat, starving. The name on the boat (is / are) the *Lady Vain*. There (was / were) blood spots on the upper edge of the vessel," he says. "You were in luck," he continues, "to get picked up by a ship that (have / has) a medical man aboard. Those who (was / were) with you did not share the same fate. Each of those creatures (have / has) perished."

AVOID FAULTY TENSE SHIFTS

When you write, don't shift tenses unless the time frame really changes. In the example below, the first sentence is a generalization, while the next three sentences are part of a past tense story.

> I **believe** in bad luck. Last Saturday, I **walked** under a ladder. Suddenly, bad things **began** to happen. First, I **slipped** while I **was carrying** a tray at work. Then I **cut** my finger.

TIP

Would and *Could*

When you tell a story about a past event, use ***would*** instead of *will* and ***could*** instead of *can*.

would / **could not**

In 1850, some doctors ~~will~~ cut patients. People ~~cannot~~ complain.

EXERCISE 6 TENSE CONSISTENCY

Underline and correct six errors involving tense shifts.

didn't

EXAMPLE: In 1938, he dieted, but he doesn't lose much weight.

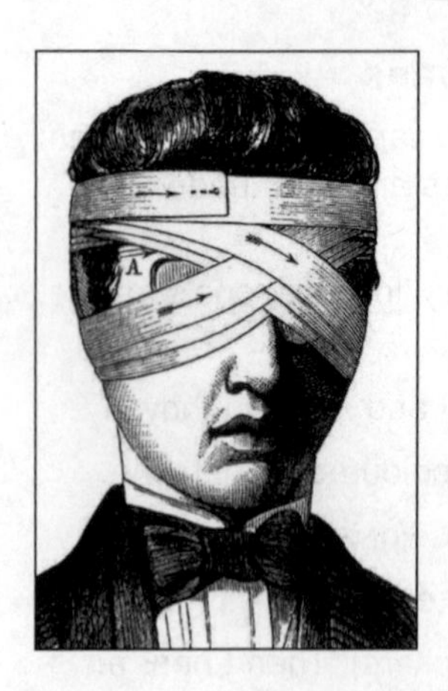

For many centuries, bloodletting and skull drilling were common medical practices. Doctors will cut patients and permit their blood to flow in the false belief that this will balance the patient's system. The practice is common until the nineteenth century. In addition, doctors had an interesting cure for migraines. They can drill small holes directly into a patient's skull. Unsurprisingly, the holes will rarely relieve a patient's headaches. Even these days, many people still chose unhealthy or suspicious remedies to cure their headaches. Perhaps in the future, some of our modern medical practices will appear ridiculous.

WRITING ABOUT FICTION

When writing about historical events, use the past tense. When writing about a fictional short story or novel, use the present tense to describe the characters and their situations.

> In the 1920s, many great writers **lived** in Paris. A classic Ernest Hemingway novel **describes** the Parisian nightlife. The main characters **meet** in cafés.

EXERCISE 7 WRITING ABOUT FICTION

Underline and correct ten errors involving tense shifts.

1. In 1929, Canadian author Morley Callaghan spends the summer in Paris. Almost every day, he will join other writers in popular cafés. Callaghan becomes friends with Ernest Hemingway. Their friendship ended after he wins a boxing match against Hemingway.

2. In Paris, Hemingway wrote *The Sun Also Rises*. The novel is about Jake Barns and his relationship with a promiscuous divorcee, Lady Brett Ashley. Ashley cuts her hair short and had modern attitudes. Barns falls in love with her, so her numerous love affairs angered him. Tensions built, and several men had fist fights with each other. Ashley chose to return to her former lover, Mike Campbell. In the final scene, Ashley and Barns were in a taxi. They are sad because they won't be together.

UNIT Review

Complete the following exercises. If you don't know an answer, go back and review the appropriate section.

1. When should you add –s or –es to verbs? ______________________

____

2. Some indefinite pronouns are singular and require the singular form of a verb. List six singular indefinite pronouns.

______________ ______________ ______________

______________ ______________ ______________

3. Some nouns are collective and require the singular form of a verb. Underline the five singular collective nouns below.

army	committee	family	police
brothers	crowd	judge	population

4. When should you use *was* or *were*?

a) Use *was* ______________________________

b) Use *were* ______________________________

→

5. Underline and correct the errors in subject-verb agreement in the following sentences.

a) There is many different religions.

b) Either the Edwards sisters or Simon are in the room.

c) One of our cousins live in Thailand.

d) The majority of the citizens has smartphones.

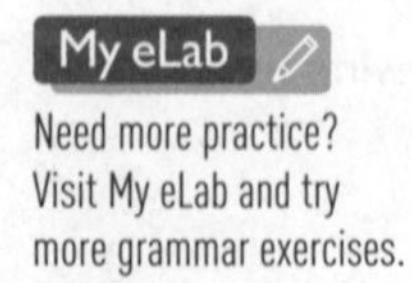

Need more practice? Visit My eLab and try more grammar exercises.

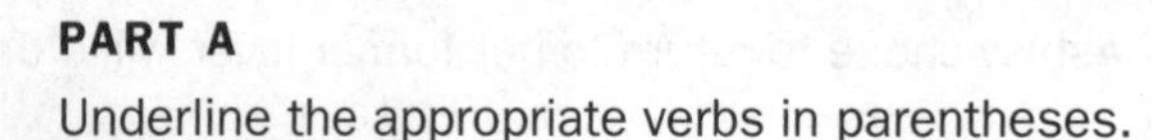

Final Review

PART A

Underline the appropriate verbs in parentheses.

1. There (is / are) many interesting survival facts. For example, if someone (encounter / encounters) a black bear, one of the worst things to do (is / are) to play dead. Although black bears rarely attack humans, the black bear (welcome / welcomes) easy prey. The majority of the population (believe / believes) that running away is the best option. However, a hungry enough bear often (chase / chases) its prey and can reach speeds of up to 50 kilometres per hour. Speaking gently and backing away slowly (is / are) the best responses. Black bears have poor eyesight. They usually retreat if they hear you speaking and realize you are a human. More than 90 percent of people (don't / doesn't) know those facts.

2. Another fact that almost nobody (know / knows) concerns riptides. A riptide is a strong current that sometimes (pull / pulls) swimmers out to sea. The majority of swimmers (try / tries) to return to shore. However, such currents are extremely strong, and it is difficult or impossible to swim against them.

3. If you are caught in a riptide, one of the most important things to remember (is / are) to remain calm. In 2009, Romilla Higgens, along with her daughter, (was / were) in shallow water. A tide pulled them out to sea. The police

(was / were) nearby, and one officer ran into the ocean. Either one or several lifeguards (was / were) also nearby. Sadly, neither Higgens nor her daughter (was / were) able to make it to safety.

4. In another case, Stephanie Hayes was swimming with her sons when a riptide began to pull them out. Luckily, each of them (was / were) aware of safety procedures. They (was / were) calm as the current pulled them away from the beach, and then they swam out of the current, to the side, instead of toward the shore. After the incident, Hayes, as well as her two sons, (was / were) safe. Everybody (need / needs) to learn about riptide safety procedures.

PART B

Underline and correct ten errors in subject-verb agreement and/or tense shifts.

5. Annually, there is more than ten thousand car-submersion accidents in North America. Apparently, during car submersions, many people panic and forgets to remove their seat belts. In addition, the majority of people tries to open the car door, but once the lower part of the door is underwater, the door was almost impossible to open. Finally, one of the biggest mistakes are when trapped drivers or passengers in cars with electric windows wait too long to open the windows. After these cars hit the water, the electric motors that operates the windows can stop working.

6. For example, in 2006, Archie Allen accidentally drove his car into the Chester River in Maryland. After the car hit the water, Allen's electric window won't open. He thought that he will die. Luckily, he can escape from a rear window and he swims to shore. He was lucky to survive.

An Admirable Person

Work with a partner. First, describe someone whom you admire. What are the person's best qualities? Give specific examples of that person's actions that are admirable. Then, listen as your partner does the same for someone he or she admires. When you finish, write a paragraph about your partner and the person that he or she has chosen.

UNIT 2

Present, Past, and Future Tenses

Preview

MEMORABLE EVENTS

Work with a partner. Choose one of the following photos of a memorable event, or choose a more recent event. On a piece of paper, do the following:

- Write five sentences to explain what happened.
- Then write six questions about the event. Write two questions concerning the past, two questions concerning the present, and two questions concerning the future.

A.

Japan
Tsunami and nuclear meltdown
March 11, 2011

B.

Quebec
Student strike
Spring 2012

Verb Tenses: Forms and Usage

PRESENT TENSES

Compare the **simple present** and the **present progressive** tenses.

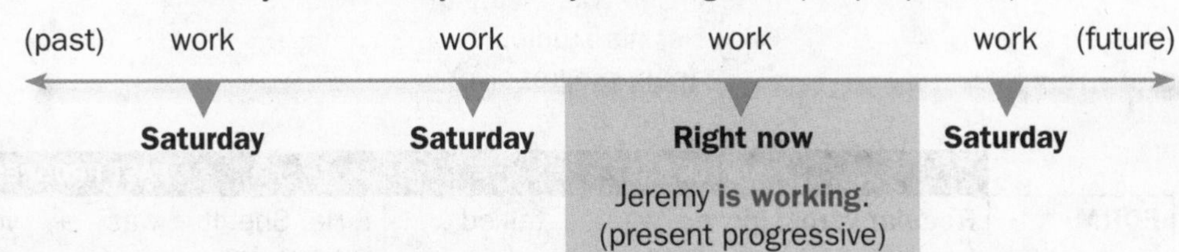

	SIMPLE PRESENT (GENERAL)	PRESENT PROGRESSIVE (NOW OR TEMPORARY PERIOD)
FORM	I, You, We, They } like. He, She, It } likes.	I am + <u>verb</u> + *–ing*. He, She, It is + <u>verb</u> + *–ing*. You, We, They are + <u>verb</u> + *–ing*.
USAGE	Indicates general truths, facts, habitual actions, and customs. Some nations **have** oil. (fact) Alicia **travels** every winter. (habit) Devout Muslims **fast** during Ramadan. (custom) **Keywords:** always, often, usually, sometimes, seldom, rarely, never, every day ...	Indicates that an action is happening now or for a present, temporary period of time. Right now, we **are eating** lunch. (now) This week, Jamil **is taking** a break. (temporary period of time) **Keywords:** now, at this moment, currently, today, these days, this week, this month, this morning ...
QUESTION	Put *do* or *does* before the subject. Use the base form of the verb. **Do** you often travel? **Does** she have a passport? **Exception:** *be* **Is** the plane late? **Are** they happy?	Put *be* before the subject. **Am** I bothering you? **Is** she sleeping now? **Are** they staying with us?
NEGATIVE	Add *do* or *does* + *not*. The train **does not** provide food. (doesn't) They **do not** own a car. (don't) **Exception:** *be* They are **not** late. (aren't)	Add *not*. He is **not** sleeping right now. (isn't) They are **not** working today. (aren't)

PAST TENSES

Compare the **simple past** and the **past progressive** tenses.

Yesterday, Khaleb **was cleaning** his studio when the fire **started**.

	SIMPLE PAST	PAST PROGRESSIVE
FORM	**Regular verbs:** looked, wanted, talked … **Irregular verbs:** ate, broke, had, saw …	I, He, She, It was + verb + *–ing*. You, We, They were + verb + *–ing*.
USAGE	The **simple past** indicates that an action was completed at a definite time in the past. Last week, we **bought** plane tickets. **Keywords:** ago, yesterday, last week, when I was a child, many years ago, once upon a time …	The **past progressive** shows that an action was in progress at a specific past time. It can also show that a past action was interrupted. Yesterday at 1 a.m., we **were sleeping**. (specific past time) While I **was eating** lunch, the phone rang. (interrupted action) **Keywords:** as, when, while, during, at 4 a.m., at noon …
QUESTION	Put *did* before the subject. Use the base form of the verb. **Did** you **travel** last year? **Did** they **help** you? **Exception:** *be* **Was** Julie late? **Were** you angry?	Put *be* before the subject. **Was** he **speaking** loudly at 1 a.m.? **Were** they **waiting** for me at noon?
NEGATIVE	Add *did* + *not*. Julie **did not** complain yesterday. (didn't) They **did not** travel last year. (didn't) **Exception:** *be* They were **not** late. (weren't)	Add *not*. He was **not** speaking loudly at 1 a.m. (wasn't) They were **not** waiting for me at noon. (weren't)

FUTURE TENSES

FORM	USAGE	EXAMPLE
will + verb	• prediction • spontaneous action or gesture of willingness	It **will rain** soon. I**'ll pay** for the meal. She**'ll do** it!
be going to + verb	• prediction • previously planned action	It **is going to rain** soon. I**'m going to leave**.

SPELLING OF VERB FORMS ENDING IN *–ING* OR *–ED*

BASE FORM	*–ING* ENDING	*–ED* ENDING	SPELLING RULES
smoke	smok**ing**	smok**ed**	***–ing*:** When verbs end in *–e*, drop the *–e* and add *–ing*. ***–ed*:** When verbs end in *–e*, simply add *–d*.
		One-Syllable Verbs	
stop	stop**ping**	stop**ped**	When one-syllable verbs end in a consonant-vowel-consonant, double the last letter and add *–ing* or *–ed*. **Exceptions:** Never double the last letter of verbs ending in *–x* or *–w* (*snowing*, *fixing*). Also, double the last letter of *quit* (*quitting*) and *quiz* (*quizzed*) even though they have two vowels; the *qu* sounds like the consonants *kw*.
		Multi-Syllable Verbs	
visit develop	visit**ing** develop**ing**	visit**ed** develop**ed**	When the final syllable is not stressed in verbs ending in a consonant-vowel-consonant, add *–ing* or *–ed*.
refer omit	refe**rring** omi**tting**	refe**rred** omi**tted**	When the final syllable is stressed in verbs ending in a consonant-vowel-consonant, double the last letter and add *–ing* or *–ed*.
		Verbs Ending in *–y* or *–ie*	
enjoy	enjoy**ing**	enjoy**ed**	When verbs end in a vowel + *–y*, just add *–ing* or *–ed*.
worry carry	worry**ing** carry**ing**	worr**ied** carr**ied**	When verbs end in a consonant + *–y*, just add *–ing*. However, when forming the past tense, change *–y* to *–i* and add *–ed*.
tie	t**ying**	tie**d**	When verbs end in *–ie*, change the *–ie* to *–y* and add *–ing*. When forming the past tense, just add *–d*.

PRONUNCIATION HELP WITH ONLINE DICTIONARIES

Many dictionaries are available online. On some sites, such as *dictionary.reference.com*, a word's stressed syllable is indicated in bold, and by clicking on the loudspeaker icon, you can hear the pronunciation of the word.

be · gin · ning [bih-**gin**-ing]

Practice

EXERCISE 1 PRESENT TENSES

Underline the correct verb forms in the parentheses below. Then identify the usage of each of these verbs. Write *G* if the verb refers to a general fact or habit. Write *N* if it refers to an action that is happening now or for a temporary period of time.

EXAMPLE: What (is she reading / does she read) __N__ right now?

1. Frequently, Brigitte Fortin (is having / have / has) ______ flashbacks to a serious car accident she was involved in. In fact, right now, she (is talking / talk / talks) ______ about it with her husband. Brigitte (is wanting / want / wants) ______ to forget about the crash, but she (isn't knowing / doesn't know /

don't knows) ______ how to do it. At this moment, she (is crying / cry / cries) ______ because she remembers how terrified she was when her brakes stopped working. Her car left the road and flipped over three times. She spent three months in the hospital. This month she (take / takes / is taking) ______ anxiety medication.

2. People rarely (are retaining / retain / retains) ______ strong memories about physical pain. If they did, women would never have more than one baby. Emotional pain and fear, however, (are lasting / last / lasts) ______ for a long time in people's minds. Today, Alex Fortin (is driving / drive / drives) ______ on a highway for the first time since his wife's accident. Right now, his wife (is talking / talk / talks) ______ to him from the passenger seat. Alex always (is driving / drive / drives) ______ carefully.

EXERCISE 2 REGULAR AND IRREGULAR PAST TENSE VERBS

Write the past tense form of the following regular and irregular verbs. (See Appendix 1 on page 149 for a list of common irregular past tense verbs.)

EXAMPLES: watch <u>watched</u> say <u>said</u>

Regular		**Irregular**	
1. spy	______	**8.** ring	______
2. stay	______	**9.** bring	______
3. rely	______	**10.** lead	______
4. employ	______	**11.** think	______
5. snap	______	**12.** drink	______
6. prefer	______	**13.** choose	______
7. mention	______	**14.** keep	______

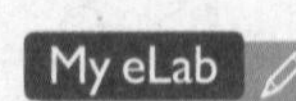

Visit My eLab for more practice spelling past tense verbs.

SIMPLE PAST AND PAST PROGRESSIVE

Use the past progressive to describe a past action that was in progress. Do not overuse the past progressive tense. Never use it to talk about past habits or a series of past actions.

Past habit: Joshua ~~was playing~~ **played** guitar when he was younger.

Series of past actions: Last night, he ~~was singing~~ **sang**, ~~was dancing~~ **danced**, and ~~was playing~~ **played** the drums.

EXERCISE 3 **PRESENT AND PAST TENSES**

Fill in the blanks with the correct form of the verbs in parentheses. Use present and past tenses, as appropriate.

EXAMPLE: In 1977, the Beverly Hills Supper Club fire (kill) killed over 150 people.

1. Nowadays, almost nobody (remember) ____________ the Station nightclub fire that (occur) ____________ in Rhode Island on February 20, 2003. The fire (be) ____________ one of the deadliest nightclub fires in America. One hundred people (lose) ____________ their lives in the blaze.

2. That night, just after 11:00 p.m., Great White, a popular rock band, (step) ____________ onto the stage. The fire (start) ____________ while the band (play) ____________ "Desert Moon." The soundproofing foam behind the drummer (begin) ____________ to burn. Initially, audience members (be) ____________ calm as the flame flickered. Maybe they (think) ____________ that the flames were part of the show.

3. A journalist who (film) ____________ the show captured people's reactions. At first, most people (move, not) ____________. They (stand) ____________ still while one man (point) ____________ frantically at the exit. Two minutes later, while the room (fill) ____________ with smoke, everyone panicked and (run) ____________ toward the front door.

4. Often during fires, people (remember, not) ____________ that buildings have several fire exits. Most people (go) ____________ toward the main entrance. On that night in 2003, the crowd (block) ____________ the front door, so people couldn't leave. Very few people (leave) ____________ by the other four exits. During a fire, it (be) ____________ important to react quickly. Even if one door is blocked, there (be) ____________ usually other ways to leave a building.

NON-PROGRESSIVE VERBS

The verbs below are not generally used in the progressive tense because they indicate an ongoing state rather than a temporary action.

PREFERENCE		STATE		POSSESSION	PERCEPTION	
admire	like	agree	realize	belong	appear*	seem
appreciate	love	believe	recognize	have*	hear	smell*
care	mind	consist	refuse	own	imagine	sound*
desire	need	cost	remember	possess	notice	taste*
despise	prefer	doubt	think*		see	weigh*
envy	want	forget	trust			
hate		know	understand			
		mean				

* Some verbs have more than one meaning and can be used in the progressive tense. Compare the following pairs of sentences.

Progressive	Non-Progressive
He **is having** a bad day.	He **has** two Picassos. (expresses possession)
I **am thinking** about money.	I **think** it is expensive. (expresses an opinion)
She **is weighing** herself.	She **weighs** 130 pounds. (expresses a fact)

EXERCISE 4 IDENTIFY ERRORS IN SIMPLE AND PROGRESSIVE VERBS

In the following sentences, underline and correct present or past tense errors. Write *C* beside sentences that are correct.

EXAMPLE: That morning, everyone <u>rest</u> (was resting) when the engine started to burn.

1. Occasionally, people are surviving plane crashes.
2. In May of 2010, a plane was crashing in Libya.
3. Why the plane crashed?
4. The plane be flying over a desert when the engine failed.
5. Why there were so many casualties?
6. Only one child did survived.
7. Amazingly, the ten-year old child had only a few leg fractures.
8. In October 2010, Libyan authorities were determining the cause of the crash.
9. They claimed that poor landing equipment and pilot error was the main causes of the crash.
10. A lot of people are not believing that flying is safe.
11. They are thinking that airplanes are dangerous.
12. Flying in an airplane is safer than driving on a highway.

SUBJECT AND OBJECT QUESTIONS

When using *who*, *what*, *how much*, or *how many* to ask about the **subject** of a question, you don't need an auxiliary.

Lena lives with Jonas.	**The car** hit a fence.	**Fifty** paintings survived.
Who lives with Jonas?	**What** hit a fence?	**How many** paintings survived?

When using *who(m)*,* *what*, *how much*, or *how many* to ask about the **object** of a question, you must add an auxiliary to the question.

Lena lived with **Jonas**.	The car hit **a fence**.	She had **fifty** paintings.
Who(m) did Lena live with?	**What did** the car hit?	**How many** paintings **did** she have?

* *Whom* is used in formal and academic English. In informal English, it is acceptable to use *who*.

EXERCISE 5 QUESTIONS

Change the following sentences into questions. Answers to the questions are in bold.

EXAMPLE: **A tsunami** hit Thailand.

What hit Thailand?

1. Tilly Smith lives **in England**.

2. She is thinking about **the past** right now.

3. She learned about tsunamis **in 2004**.

4. She went **to Phuket**.

5. Her family stayed in a hotel **for three weeks**.

6. She knew **a tsunami was coming**.

7. She warned **her parents** about the tsunami.

8. **Tilly** saved many people.

9. She asked **a guard** to evacuate the beach.

→

10. She wanted people to leave the beach **because she recognized the warning signs of a coming tsunami**.

____

11. People **were running** when the giant waves arrived.

____

12. **The hotel lobby** became full of rushing water.

____

13. **Hundreds** of people survived.

____

14. She will return to Thailand **next summer**.

____

15. She is going to stay **at the same hotel**.

____

FUTURE TENSES

Use *will* or *be going to* when you predict the future. For previously planned actions, use *be going to*. For spontaneous actions, use *will*.

Prediction:	The population **will grow**. It **is going to explode**.
Planned:	I found a job. I **am going to work** in London.
Spontaneous:	The doorbell is ringing. I **will answer** it.

TIP

Present Tenses

Sometimes the present tenses can refer to a future time. The **present progressive** can refer to a previously planned event that will happen soon. The **simple present** can refer to schedules and timetables.

We **are leaving** tonight. The show **starts** in two hours.

EXERCISE 6 **FUTURE TENSES**

Fill in the blanks with the appropriate future tense form of the verbs in parentheses. Note that in some instances, there is more than one possible answer.

EXAMPLE: If you are having problems, I (help) will help you.

1. Noah: In the election, who (you, vote) _______________ for?
2. Anna: I'm not sure. Maybe I (support) _______________ the left-leaning candidate. On the other hand, she (raise) _______________ _______________ taxes. At least, she said she would in her campaign literature.

3. Noah: Perhaps she has to. How (we, pay) ______________________ for rising health care costs?

4. Anna: Please don't try to influence me. Maybe I just (vote, not) ______________________. My vote probably (make, not) ______________________ a difference, anyway.

5. Noah: Don't think that way. Listen, I (watch) ______________________ the debate tonight. Why don't you watch it with me?

6. Anna: I can't. My train (leave) ______________________ at 8 p.m.

7. Noah: Your train left ten minutes ago! Wait here while I get my keys. I (drive) ______________________ you home.

TIME CLAUSES IN FUTURE TENSE SENTENCES

A time clause begins with a **time marker** such as those below. When describing the future, use the present tense after the time marker.

after	as soon as	before	unless	until
as long as	in case	when	whatever	whenever

The time marker can appear in the first or second part of the sentence.

After I **finish** college, I **will travel**.
Caleb **will call** us as soon as he **arrives**.

TIP

Never Write *Gonna*

Although people say *gonna*, it isn't a proper word. Always write *going to*.

I'm ~~gonna~~ **going to** finish this project.

EXERCISE 7 FUTURE TENSES AND TIME CLAUSES

PART A

Circle the time markers in the sentences below. Then underline and correct all verb errors.

EXAMPLE: I will leave (as soon as) I will finish [finish] my work.

1. When the spring will arrive, will there be any floods?

2. Tomorrow, the roads will be slippery after the freezing rain will come.

→

3. As soon as the sea levels will rise, there will be a lot of flooding.

4. Other problems will occur unless nations will reduce their greenhouse gases.

5. After the election is over and some time will pass, will the situation change?

PART B

Underline and correct five errors involving future tenses.

6. Scientists predict that major earthquakes will occur on the Pacific coast of North America. What are citizens gonna do? How big the next earthquake going to be? When such disasters will occur, will the coastline change? Where residents are going to live after a catastrophe? Unless engineers and construction companies will work together to build more earthquake-proof structures, many buildings and bridges will probably collapse.

AVOIDING DOUBLE NEGATIVES

Double negatives contain two negative words that cancel each other out. To correct double negatives, either remove one of the two negative forms, or change *no* to *any*.

Double Negative	Possible Corrections
She **doesn't** have **no** children.	She doesn't have children. (Remove *no*.) She has no children. (Remove *doesn't*.) She doesn't have any children. (Change *no* to *any*.)

EXERCISE 8 **IDENTIFY ERRORS**

Underline and correct the errors in the sentences below. Write *C* beside the sentences that are correct.

EXAMPLE: Yesterday, in class, did you heard (hear) about the dog who survived on a deserted island?

1. A few years ago, Jan Griffth decided to took a boat ride with her dog Sophie.

2. When Sophie fell overboard, Jan didn't have no idea if the dog was dead or alive.

3. What did happen to the dog?

4. The dog swam across six miles of shark-infested water to survived.

5. Sophie swam all the way to a tiny island.

6. Jan didn't think nobody was going to find her dog.

7. Amazingly, while rangers were walking on the beach, they were finding the dog.

8. Most people are agreeing that it is extremely rare for a dog to survive in shark-infested waters.

9. Jan will probably panic if she will take another boat ride.

10. Today, Jan doesn't own Sophie no more because the dog passed away a few years ago.

UNIT Review

Complete the following exercises. If you don't know an answer, go back and review the appropriate section.

1. Underline and correct the errors in the sentences below. Then explain why the sentences were incorrect.

   EXAMPLE: Every day, he is complaining about something. complains
   Rule: Don't use the present progressive with habitual actions.

   a) Last year, I was working every weekend. ______
   Rule: ______

   b) Last year, did you studied a second language? ______
   Rule: ______

   c) Vince wanted to talked with you. ______
   Rule: ______

   d) He will arrive when he will finish work. ______
   Rule: ______

   e) We don't need no education. ______
   Rule: ______

2. Write the simple past forms of the following verbs.

   EXAMPLE: bring brought

   a) fall ______ c) teach ______
   b) sing ______ d) think ______

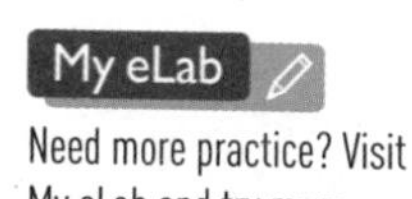

Need more practice? Visit My eLab and try more exercises about verb tenses.

Final Review

PART A

Write the correct form of each verb in parentheses. Use past, present, or future tenses.

EXAMPLE: Some plane crashes (be, not) aren't necessarily fatal.

1. My mother (like, not) ______________ to be in an airplane. In fact, many people are afraid of flying. Why (they, refuse) ______________ ______________ to fly? When you (save) ______________ enough money, will you fly in an airplane?
2. Although flying is safer than driving, accidents can occur. In 1960, the members of the Minneapolis Lakers NBA squad (have) ______________ a dangerous journey on a Butler Aviation aircraft. During a period of turbulence, while the athletes (play) ______________ cards, the lights inside the plane suddenly (go) ______________ out. The plane (become) ______________ very cold.

3. What (the pilots, do) ______________? They (be) ______________ calm. There was a lot of ice and frost on the windshield, and the plane (have, not) ______________ ______________ a defroster. The pilots couldn't see the ground easily. They (know) ______________ that they would have to land as soon as possible. With each passing minute, the plane (run) ______________ out of fuel. Their navigational systems were down, so, using physical clues instead, they (find) ______________ a safe place to land.
4. The NBA team members (be, not) ______________ sure if they would survive. Fifteen minutes later, the plane crashed in an Iowa cornfield. Amazingly, the crew and passengers (die, not) ______________.

PART B

Underline and correct five errors involving verb tenses or double negatives.

EXAMPLE: The men didn't took precautions. (take)

5. The players didn't know nothing about the plane's true situation. The pilots were wanting to find an adequate place to land the plane. The passengers was really lucky that they were alive: about 60 metres in front of the plane, there was a deep gorge! Today, Butler Aviation doesn't exist no more. In the future, when I will fly, I will appreciate the pilots.

PART C

Change the following sentences into questions. Answers to the questions are in bold.

EXAMPLE: He is talking about **the Lakers**.
Who is he talking about?

6. The pilot wanted to postpone the flight **because of poor weather conditions**.

____

7. The pilot was **resting** when the lights went out.

____

8. The movie will be about **the accident**.

____

9. He flies **every month**.

____

10. They are discussing **the movie** right now.

____

Vivid Verbs

With a partner, brainstorm to come up with ten verbs that describe very specific actions. Examples of specific verbs are *whimper*, *sniffle*, *slurp*, and *wrestle*. Refer to your *Avenues 3: English Skills* book or use your dictionary to find good examples of verbs. Write your complete list on a sheet of paper. Then exchange sheets with another team. You and your partner must then write a paragraph incorporating the other team's list of ten verbs. Use the present, past, and future tenses in your paragraph.

UNIT 3 Present Perfect Tenses

Preview

LIE DETECTOR

Write three sentences about yourself. Two of the sentences should describe true things that you have done in your life. One of your sentences should describe a lie. Later, you will pretend that you have also done that action. Do not indicate which sentence is a lie. For example, consider the following sentences:

I have danced on a street.	(true)
I have travelled to Brazil.	(false)
I have taken singing classes.	(true)

Show the sentences to a small team of fellow students. You must pretend that all of the sentences are true. Then, your classmates will ask you questions to discover which sentence is a lie. Invent answers for the false story. The team will then have to guess which sentence is true.

Statement 1: ______________________________

Statement 2: ______________________________

Statement 3: ______________________________

Present Perfect: Forms and Usage

Combine a past participle with *have* or *has* to form the present perfect tense. You can use this tense in two different circumstances:

1. To indicate that an action began in the past and continues to the present time.

2008 Leo began his job. — **Now** Leo still works here.

Leo **has worked** here since 2008.
(The event began in 2008 and continues to the present time.)

Keywords: never, ever, not yet, so far, up to now, since, for ...

2. To indicate that one or more completed past actions occurred at unspecified past times.

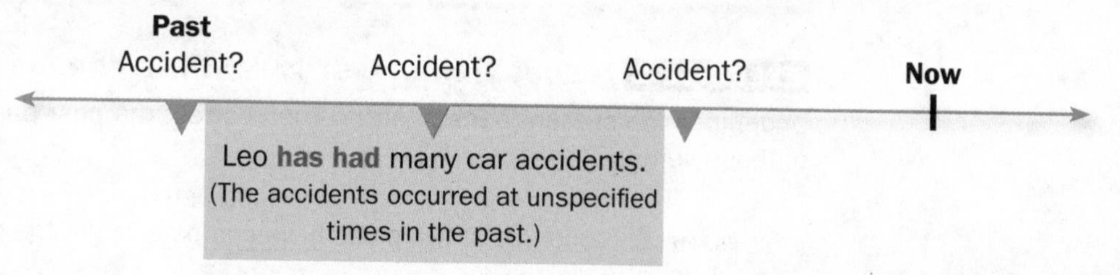

PRESENT PERFECT FORMS

FORM	I / You / We / They } **have** + past participle (eaten, seen, etc.)	He / She / It } **has** + past participle (gone, broken, etc.)
QUESTION	Move the auxiliary (*have* or *has*) before the subject. **Have** you ever **met** Donald?	**Has** Joe **been** to China?
NEGATIVE	Put *not* after *have* or *has*. I **have not met** Donald. (haven't)	Joe **has not been** to China. (hasn't)

SINCE, *FOR*, AND *AGO*

Since refers to a specific past moment when the action began.
For refers to the amount of time that the action has lasted.
Ago refers to a time in the past when the completed action occurred. Use *ago* with the past tense only.

Luis **has lived** in Calgary **since** 2008. (He is still living there.)

He **has worked** as a dentist **for** three years. (He still works as a dentist.)

He **married** Kara six years **ago**.

PRESENT PERFECT PROGRESSIVE TENSE

The present perfect progressive indicates that an action has been in progress from a past time up to the present moment. It emphasizes the *duration* of the uninterrupted activity.

Form: *have/has been* + base form of verb + *–ing*

Rajiv **has been singing** for twenty minutes. When will he stop singing?

With some verbs (e.g., *live*, *work*, *teach*, *study*), the present perfect and the present perfect progressive forms have essentially the same meaning. Compare the following sentences:

Rajiv **has been working** full-time since 2010. }
Rajiv **has worked** full-time since 2010. } Same meaning

Practice

EXERCISE 1 **RECOGNIZING PAST PARTICIPLE ERRORS**

Underline nine present perfect verbs. Then correct the past participle errors in six of those verbs.

EXAMPLE: Since 2010, two cities have compete [competed] to get the government contract.

1. Many Canadians have thinked about their cultural identity. They have questioned what it means to be Canadian. Sometimes, people in one region have fight against those in another. For example, there have been rivalries between Toronto and Montreal or between Edmonton and Calgary. In 2007, Canadian filmmaker Albert Nerenberg produced a film called *Let's All Hate Toronto*. Have you ever heared of that film?

2. What do people around the globe think about Canadians? Our hockey players have win respect. Canada has produced fine actors and comedians. Directors such as David Cronenberg have maked internationally recognized films. Canadians have also gain a reputation for being nice and self-effacing. Author Douglas Coupland once said, "Canadians can easily pass for Americans as long as we don't accidentally use metric measurements or apologize when hit by a car."

USING AN AUXILIARY WITH *HAVE*

In the present perfect tense, even when the main verb is *have*, you must still use the auxiliary *have* or *has*. Then use the past participle form of the main verb, *had*.

Matt **has had** several car accidents.
We **have had** many discussions about his driving.

EXERCISE 2 SIMPLE PAST AND PRESENT PERFECT

Fill in the blanks using the verbs and tenses indicated.

PART A SIMPLE PAST: THE ACTION WAS OVER AT A KNOWN PAST TIME.

EXAMPLE: David and William Horsley (film) Hollywood's first movie. filmed

1. Before the movie industry arrived, Hollywood (be) a quiet suburb. ____________
2. Filmmakers (avoid) strict patent laws by relocating to Hollywood. ____________
3. The Nestor company (open) the first movie studio in Hollywood. ____________
4. In the 1930s, there (be) five major studios in Hollywood. ____________

PART B PRESENT PERFECT: THE ACTION BEGAN IN THE PAST AND CONTINUES TO THE PRESENT.

EXAMPLE: Over ninety years (pass) since the film industry began. have passed

5. Since the 1920s, studios (try) to create hit films. ____________
6. People (have) dreams about fame ever since. ____________
7. The Hollywood Walk of Fame (exist) since 1927. ____________
8. For almost one hundred years, tourists (visit) Hollywood. ____________

PART C PRESENT PERFECT: ONE OR MORE ACTIONS OCCURRED AT UNKNOWN PAST TIMES.

EXAMPLE: I (see) many great films. have seen

9. Millions of people (walk) on Sunset Boulevard. ____________
10. Over the years, many films (have) stereotypical villains. ____________
11. Ryan Reynolds (be) in many popular films. ____________
12. Canada (produce) a lot of great film directors. ____________

LOOKING AT KEYWORDS

Use keywords to help you decide what tense to use. Be careful: when the past time is stated and other sentences give details about that past time, use the past tense.

Padma Kumar **has been** a set designer **since** she graduated from college. Four years **ago**, she **moved** to England. She **stayed** in a small youth hostel in London, and she **went** to several plays.

TIP

Since and *For*

Since refers to a specific past moment when the action began. ***For*** refers to the amount of time that the action has lasted.

He has lived here **since** May. I've known him **for** three months.

EXERCISE 3 **SIMPLE PAST OR PRESENT PERFECT**

PART A

Complete the following sentences using either the past or the present perfect tense of the verb. In each case, underline the keywords or phrases that indicate which tense should be used.

EXAMPLE: We (see) have seen a lot of movies this year.

1. Over the years, Hollywood films (present) ______________ many stereotypes. From the 1920s to the 1970s, Caucasian actors often (portray) ______________ Africans and Asians. Cowboy movies were often the worst. During the mid-20th century, Caucasians in redface makeup (pretend) ______________ to be Native Americans.

2. Over sixty years ago, Truman Capote (write) ______________ the well-received book *Breakfast at Tiffany's* about a country girl who moves to Manhattan. In the story, a photographer, Mr. Yunioshi, lives upstairs from her. In 1961, Hollywood (release) ______________ a movie that was based on the novel. At that time, most people (think) ______________ that the movie was excellent. But ever since its debut, the film (receive, also) ______________ criticism. In the film, a small white actor plays the role of Mr. Yunioshi. The actor wears yellowface makeup and large fake teeth. Ever since 1961, the movie (be) ______________ a prime example of stereotyping in Hollywood films.

3. Since the mid-1970s, studios (make) ______________ fewer mistakes of this sort. But some films still rely on stereotypes. For instance, in the 1990s, lawyers (be) ______________ often the bad guys in movies. And for the last few years, many films (have) ______________ Middle Eastern villains.

PART B

Complete the definitions and examples below using *since*, *for*, or *ago*.

4. _____________ refers to a past time when the action was completed. For example, "The movie hit theatres three months _____________."

5. _____________ refers to a specific past moment when the action began. The action continues to the present time. For example, "Luc has been a professional actor _____________ 2010."

6. _____________ refers to a period of time. For example, "We've been waiting in line _____________ three hours."

My eLab

For more practice using *since*, *for*, and *ago*, visit My eLab.

REVIEW THE SIMPLE PAST AND PRESENT PERFECT FORMS

Look at the differences between the past and present perfect tenses.

Present Perfect
Times are unknown.
Keywords: once, twice, many times ...
? ? ?

Specific Past Time

Now

Present Perfect
Past action continues to the present time.
Keywords: since, for ...

Simple Past
Past time is known.
Keywords: ago, last week, yesterday ...

Simple past: In 2003, Rihanna **left** Barbados for the first time.
(The event occurred at a known past time.)

Present perfect: She **has sung** since she was three years old.
(The action began in the past and continues to the present.)

She **has returned** to Barbados many times.
(We do not know each date that she visited the country.)

EXERCISE 4 **IDENTIFYING REASONS FOR TENSE USAGE**

Fill in the blanks with either the present perfect or simple past tense of the verbs. Then explain your choices.

EXAMPLE: Paul (live) with me since March. has lived

Reason: The action began in the past (March) and continues to the present.

1. Paul (go) to Cyprus last May. _____________

Reason: _____________

→

2. In Cyprus, Turks and Greeks (fight) for hundreds of years. ____________

Reason: ____________

3. Paul (visit) many countries since 2005. ____________

Reason: ____________

4. He (move) to Kingston three years ago. ____________

Reason: ____________

5. Paul and Keira (live) in Kingston since then. ____________

Reason: ____________

PAST TENSE REMINDER

Use the past tense when referring to someone who is no longer living or to an event that occurred at a known past time. Use the present perfect tense only when the action refers to someone or something that still exists.

Early humans ~~have carved~~ **carved** arrows out of stone.
Weapons **have evolved** over the years.

EXERCISE 5 SIMPLE PAST OR PRESENT PERFECT

Fill in the blanks with the simple past or present perfect form of the verbs.

EXAMPLE: Dr. Aboud (study) has studied many different children.

1. Thousands of years ago, ancient humans (feel) ____________ suspicious of people from other tribes. They (build) ____________ stone weapons that they (use) ____________ to attack each other. But since the first humans walked on Earth, people (also, develop) ____________ the ability to cooperate and to overlook differences. Can people overcome racial prejudice? Over the years, many psychologists and sociologists (study) ____________ this issue.

2. According to psychology professor Frances Aboud, "Discrimination is wired into the brain at conception." Since 1975, she (specialize) ____________ in research on childhood racial awareness. She (perform) ____________ many different studies. Over the years, she (test) ____________ thousands of children. During the 1980s, she (run) ____________

__________________ a simple test: she (show) __________________ children pairs of drawings of either boys or girls that were identical except for skin tone. Then she asked questions such as "Who is mean?" or "Who is nice?" During her tests, about 60 percent of five-year-olds (attribute) __________________ negative traits to people of colours different from their own. Aboud says that eight is "the age of reason," when children discover that there are other perspectives and that people of all colours can be both positive and negative.

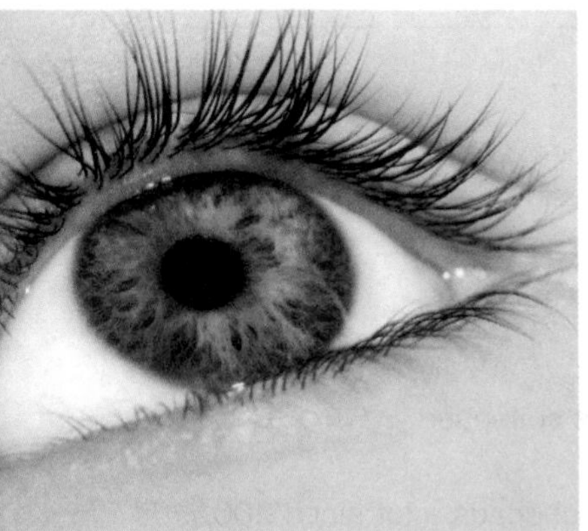

3. Aboud states that tolerance can be learned more through actions than through words. For instance, Aboud (travel) ____________ ____________________ to over thirty different nations, and she (interview) ____________________ thousands of people. She says, "When someone (have) ____________________ many experiences working intimately with those of other races, that person stops caring about skin tone." In 1988, Aboud (publish) ____________________ her first book, *Children and Prejudice*. Since then, she (write) ____________________ several other books about her research.

QUESTION WORDS

Have you ever ...?

Use this form to determine if something happened at an indefinite past time. Use *never* to specify that something hasn't occurred in a person's life.

Have you ever been to Chile? No, I have **never** been there.

How long ...?

Use this form to determine the period of time that an action lasted.

How long has Ms. Malone been the mayor? She has been the mayor for six years.

How many (times) ...?

Use this form to ask about the repetition of an activity.

How many times have you been to Portugal? I've been there twice.

TIP

Yet

Generally, use the present perfect with *yet*.

Has Jake left **yet**?

EXERCISE 6 WRITE QUESTIONS

Change the following sentences into questions. Answers to the questions are in bold.

EXAMPLE: **No,** I have never met her.
Have you ever met her?

1. Dr. Aboud has tested **hundreds** of children.

____

→

2. She has worked with that child **for three years**.

____

3. **No**, she has never lived in the United States.

____

4. She has published **more than forty** research papers.

____

5. **No**, she hasn't retired yet.

____

EXERCISE 7 **IDENTIFY ERRORS**

Underline and correct the errors in the following sentences. Look for mistakes in verb tense or with the usage of *since* and *for*. Write *C* beside the sentences that are correct.

EXAMPLE: Have you ever <u>saw</u> a drone? (seen)

1. In 2001, New York's World Trade Center has collapsed.

2. According to journalist R. Fulford, the world changes a lot since 2001.

3. Since then, North Americans had have a more militant attitude.

4. In June 2012, a pilotless remote-controlled aircraft has dropped a bomb on a house in Pakistan.

5. Since the last few years, our society has become less tolerant.

6. Fulford travelled to the United States many times.

7. Last March 9, he went through airport security.

8. That day, security guards has searched his bags thoroughly.

9. Since 2001, people have change the ways that they communicate.

10. Smart-phone technology have improved since 2008.

11. Since several years, I have used Skype to call my cousin.

12. I buy many different cellphones over the years.

13. How long you have had a phone?

14. For three years, my brother owns an iPhone.

EXERCISE 8 PAST, PRESENT PERFECT, AND PRESENT PERFECT PROGRESSIVE

Fill in the blanks with the past, present perfect, or present perfect progressive form of the verbs. (To review the present perfect progressive tense, see page 27.)

1. Christian (be) ____________________ a war photographer for many years. He wants to publish a book of photographs. He (send) ____________________ proposals to several publishers. He (wait) ________________________ for a response for three months.
2. Another friend, Sun Hee, is also a photographer. She (take) ____________________ hundreds of amazing black-and-white portraits. Last week, she (decide) ____________________ to publish a book about tolerance. She will try to sell it on Amazon. For the last six hours, she (work) ____________________________ non-stop on her project, and her husband (sleep) _______________ ____________________ because it is the middle of the night.

UNIT Review

Complete the following exercises. If you don't know an answer, go back and review the appropriate section.

1. When do you use the present perfect tense? Give two explanations.
   a) ____
   b) ____
2. Underline and correct the verb-tense errors in the following sentences. Then write a rule to explain your corrections.
   a) Heather O'Neill has published her first book in 2006. _______________
      Rule: ____
   b) Her book won many awards. _______________
      Rule: ____
   c) She has been a famous writer since several years. _______________
      Rule: ____
   d) She has wrote more than fifty poems. _______________
      Rule: ____
   e) For ten years, we have a dog. We love our dog. _______________
      Rule: ____

My eLab

Need more practice? Visit My eLab and try more exercises on verb tenses.

Final Review

PART A

Fill in the blanks with the simple past or present perfect form of the verbs in parentheses.

EXAMPLE: I (see, never) have never seen a Muppets movie.

1. Filmmakers often create stereotypes because it is a simple way to establish a movie character's traits. For instance, the dumb blonde is a stereotype. During most of the last century, movie directors (care, not) ______________________ if their movies had racist elements. But for the last thirty years, most directors (try) ______________________ to avoid stereotypical representations. However, someone will always dislike the choice of a movie's bad guy, who is often society's current villain. For instance, during World War II, movie villains were often German. In 2009, the directors of *The Muppets* (choose) ________________ the Texas oil tycoon, Tex Richman, as the villain. Ever since the film's release in 2011, the use of the "evil oil tycoon" character (cause) ____________________ some controversy.

2. In 2011, a popular news anchor from Fox Television (complain) ______________________ bitterly about the Muppets movie. In fact, he (say) ____________________ that the movie was "pushing a dangerous liberal agenda and trying to brainwash children." Then, on April 2, 2012, a woman from Bee Cave, Texas, (phone) ____________________ Rush Limbaugh's radio show. During the call, she (yell) ____________________ about the movies *Cars* and *The Muppets*. Both films (sell) ____________________ a lot of tickets since their debuts. Holly, the Texan caller, said, "I (have) ____________________ several bad experiences at the movies since the early 2000s. Over the last few years, my children (see) ________________ some negative images of people who work in the oil industry. Many times, I (explain) __________________________ to them that their father's job isn't evil."

3. When the controversy first (begin) ____________________, the producers of *The Muppets* were amused. In January 2012, the characters of Kermit

the Frog and Miss Piggy (hold) ____________________ a news conference to defend their film. Since then, there (be) ____________________ several funny YouTube videos about the incident.

PART B

Underline and correct the verb-tense errors in the following sentences. Write *C* beside the sentences that are correct.

4. In the early 1960s, Marilyn Monroe has been one of Hollywood's most popular actresses.

5. Since the 1920s, hundreds of movies have include the "dumb blonde."

6. During her lifetime, Marilyn Monroe hated her "dumb blonde" image and has tried to change it.

7. Since Monroe's death, biographers discovered that she was actually very intelligent.

8. Have you ever watch a Marilyn Monroe movie?

Interview with a Famous Person

Work with a partner, and think about someone you both admire. It could be a well-known actor, scientist, athlete, musician, entrepreneur, or politician. After you have chosen someone, then imagine that you have the opportunity to interview that person. Write ten questions that you would ask him or her. Use a variety of verb tenses, and use the present perfect tense at least three times.

UNIT 4

Past Perfect and Future Perfect Tenses

Preview

WHO DID IT?

Can you identify the differences between the simple past and the past perfect tenses? Read each group of sentences below and answer the questions that follow.

1. When the fire occurred, Mick had left the building.
   When the fire occurred, Rene left the building.
   Question: Who inhaled some smoke? ____________________
2. When Tomas went to the London Olympics, he had won a gold medal.
   When Nicolas went to the London Olympics, he won a gold medal.
   Question: Who was already a gold-medal winner when he got to the London Olympics? ____________________
3. Last night at 9 p.m., Lia had taken her dog for a walk.
   Last night at 9 p.m., Jonathan took his dog for a walk.
   Question: Whose dog went for a walk before 9 p.m.? ____________________
4. Kendra had eaten when Gabriel invited her to dinner.
   Sara ate when Gabriel invited her to dinner.
   Question: Who was not hungry when Gabriel invited her to dinner? ____________________

Past Perfect Tenses: Forms and Usage

PAST PERFECT

The past perfect tense indicates that one past action happened before another past action.

The movie **had** already **started** when Jasmine arrived.

Past — The movie started. — Jasmine arrived. — **Now**

Keywords: already, up to that time, by then ...

PAST PERFECT PROGRESSIVE

The past perfect progressive indicates that an action was in progress (without interruption) before another past action occurred.

When I returned home, I realized that somebody **had been using** my computer. It was still warm.

Past I arrived. **Now**

Somebody **had been using** my computer before I arrived.

PAST PERFECT FORMS

FORM	Subject + *had* + past participle (eaten, seen, etc.) They **had completed** the project when I was hired.
QUESTION	Move the auxiliary (*had*) before the subject. What **had** she **done** before you arrived?
NEGATIVE	Add *not* after *had*. I **had not** (hadn't) **eaten** when the restaurant closed.
PROGRESSIVE	In the **past perfect progressive**, use *had been* + gerund (*–ing* form of the verb) to describe an action that had been continually in progress up to a specific past time. When I lost my job, I **had been working** at the company for ten years.

Note: When *before* or *after* is used in a sentence, the past perfect is not always necessary because the time relationship is already clear. Consider the following:

Past perfect: The movie **had ended**, so I left the theatre.

You could also use the simple past: After the movie **ended**, I left the theatre.

Future Perfect Tense: Forms and Usage

Use the future perfect tense to indicate that an action will occur before or up to a future time or future action.

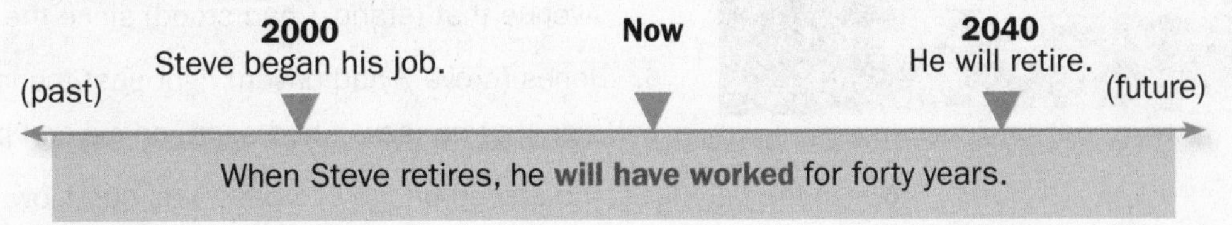

Keywords: by the time, by next year, by then, by Monday, by the weekend ...

FUTURE PERFECT FORMS

FORM	Subject + *will have* + past participle (gone, done, etc.) By next month, I **will have had** three operations.
QUESTION	Move the auxiliary (*will*) before the subject. How long **will** she **have worked**?
NEGATIVE	Put *not* between *will* and *have*. By next summer, I **will not** (won't) **have finished** my degree.
PROGRESSIVE	In the **future perfect progressive**, use *will have been* + *–ing* form of the verb to describe an action that will have been continually in progress up to a specific future time or action. When I retire, I **will have been working** for forty years.

Practice

EXERCISE 1 PAST AND PAST PERFECT

For each sentence, underline the correct form of the verb in parentheses.

EXAMPLE: When James Anthony Jones drove a group of students to George Washington's home, he (already worked / <u>had already worked</u>) as a bus driver for many years.

1. In 2004, bus driver James Anthony Jones had to drive a group of students to George Washington's house, a trip he (made / had made) many times.
2. By the time Jones started driving, he felt angry because the lead driver in another bus (insulted / had insulted) him.
3. While driving, Jones (called / had called) his sister and told her that he (never liked / had never liked) the other driver.
4. En route, there (was / had been) a bridge on Alexandria Avenue that (stand / had stood) since the early 1930s.
5. Jones (drove / had driven) right past the large yellow warning sign that he (saw / had seen) on several previous occasions.
6. In the right lane, the arched bridge overpass was quite low, but in the centre lane, it (was / had been) high enough for a truck to pass under.
7. The lead bus (already moved / had already moved) to the middle lane when Jones (arrived / had arrived) at the bridge.

8. Jones's bus (smashed / had smashed) forcefully into the bridge, and the collision (destroyed / had destroyed) the roof of the bus.
9. Investigators determined that Jones (tried / had tried) to multi-task by driving and speaking on a cellphone at the same time.
10. Later, Jones told investigators that he (didn't see / hadn't seen) the bridge.

EXERCISE 2 **IDENTIFY TENSE ERRORS**

Underline and correct ten verb-tense errors. Look for errors in any tense.

EXAMPLE: Marcia called a journalist and then <u>had described</u> (described) the accident.

1. On March 15, 2012, Yuzu Noda was tour Australia with two of her friends. They have never been to Australia before. At 11 a.m., they were driving beside a lake. Earlier, Noda had program the destination of a nearby island into her GPS. When the GPS said, "Turn right," Noda had turned the wheel and drove into the lake. After the accident, Noda was blaming her GPS. She argued that the machine had told her to turn. One of Noda's passengers later texted that she was never so scared in her life.

2. Apparently, people often are having accidents because they rely too much on their GPS devices. In another case, in June 2011, three women in Seattle were driving a Mercedes SUV that they have rented. The car's GPS suggested that they turn onto a boat launch ramp, so the driver drove onto it. By the time the driver realized her error, the car sunk into the water. Of course, the woman had to pay an insurance penalty because she has damaged the car.

PAST PERFECT PROGRESSIVE

Use the past perfect progressive to indicate that an action was in progress (without interruption) before another past action occurred.

It **had been raining** for about ten minutes when lightning struck the house.

EXERCISE 3 **PAST FORMS**

Fill in the blanks with the simple past, past progressive, past perfect, or past perfect progressive form of the verbs in parentheses, as appropriate.

EXAMPLE: When Wilson (arrive) arrived, Marino (cook) had been cooking for hours.

1. Last summer, when Art Wilson was in Venice, something strange (happen) ______________________. He stopped in front of a small empty restaurant, and he could see an old woman who (cook) ______________________ at the stove. She was stirring soup. Suddenly, he had the feeling that he (be) ______________________ there before. The shop owner, Rosina Marino, went outside because the strange man (look) ______________________ at her for about five minutes. Wilson told her about his strong sense of déjà vu. He (feel) ______________________ like he (be) ______________________ there before, even though he (visit, never) ______________________ Venice.

2. Marino and Wilson (talk) ______________________ for a few minutes. Suddenly, they were thrown to the ground. The restaurant's gas stove (explode, just) ______________________. A few minutes earlier, Marino (stand) ______________________ at that stove. Wilson never learned why he (have) ______________________ that sense of déjà vu, but he was grateful that his feeling (save) ______________________ someone's life.

FUTURE PERFECT, PERFECT PROGRESSIVE, AND PROGRESSIVE

Use the **future perfect** to indicate that an action will occur before or up to a future time or future action.

The **future perfect progressive** shows that an action will be in progress up to a future time or action.

Future perfect:	Next summer, Zac **will have been** a student for exactly twenty years.
Future perfect progressive:	By Sunday, I **will have been working** for thirty hours non-stop on this project.

The **future progressive** indicates that an action will be in progress at a specific future time.

When you call me tomorrow, I **will be working**.

EXERCISE 4 FUTURE PERFECT, PERFECT PROGRESSIVE, AND PROGRESSIVE FORMS

Fill in the blanks with the future perfect, future perfect progressive, or future progressive form of the verbs in parentheses, as appropriate.

EXAMPLE: Tomorrow evening at 9 p.m., don't disturb me because I (study) will be studying. By next Tuesday, I (spend) will have spent three weeks preparing for the test.

1. I have a huge art project to do. It is 5 p.m., but I must finish it. Tonight at midnight, I (work, still) ______________________ on it. I hope that I will finish by Sunday. Don't call me on Sunday. I'm planning to sleep all day. If you call at noon, I (sleep) ______________________. By the time I finish the project, I (spend) ______________________ over eighty hours on it. When I finish my fine-arts degree next June, I (be) ______________________ a university student for four years.
2. On Monday, my sister is coming to visit. I work until 10:00 p.m., but my sister's bus arrives at 9 p.m. When I go to pick up my sister, her bus (arrive) ______________________, and she (wait) ______________________ for me for about an hour by the time I get there. But there is nothing I can do about it. She will have to wait.

UNIT Review

Complete the following exercises. If you don't know an answer, go back and review the appropriate section.

1. Underline three past perfect verbs and circle one future perfect verb.

were sleeping	had visited	have done	has seen	will have done
had tried	has gone	was	had had	will be doing

2. Underline and correct one error involving verb tense in each sentence.

   a) When I arrived at the party, my hosts had already finish dinner.

   b) Why they had already eaten?

   c) I left the party and went to Maria's, but when I arrived at her house, she had went out.

   d) Tonight, by the time I go to bed, I will be awake for twenty hours.

My eLab

Need more practice? Visit My eLab and try additional exercises.

Final Review

Fill in the blanks with the appropriate form of the verbs in parentheses. You can use any form of the present, past, or future tenses.

EXAMPLE: In past centuries, kings and queens (have) had tremendous power.

1. These days in our history class, we (learn) ____________________ about ancient Egypt. So far, we (have) ____________________ six quizzes. Tomorrow, when I (arrive) ____________________ in class, my professor will give us a two-hour exam on ancient Egypt.
2. In 55 BC, when the king of Egypt (die) ____________________, the Egyptian people (expect) ____________________ his death for many months. A few days later, the king's seventeen-year-old daughter, Cleopatra, (become) ____________________ the queen of Egypt, and then she (marry) ____________________ her brother, Ptolemy, according to ancient tradition.
3. Three years later, when Julius Caesar (enter) ____________________ Egypt, Ptolemy arranged a visit with the Roman ruler, but he excluded his sister. Cleopatra wanted to be a part of any deals, so she (plan) ____________________ to meet Caesar too. She (hide) ____________________ inside a rug and was delivered to Caesar's room.

4. Cleopatra (seduce) ____________________ Caesar. He told Cleopatra that he (see, never) ____________________ such a beautiful woman. When he first (hear) ____________________ her sing, he insisted that he (never, hear) ____________________ such a sweet voice. That night, while the couple (whisper) ____________________ in bed, Cleopatra (convince) ____________________ Caesar to make her the sole ruler of Egypt.
5. The next morning, Ptolemy arrived in Caesar's room and (realize) ____________________ that Cleopatra (meet, already) ____________________ the foreign ruler. Ptolemy was furious and he (shout) ____________________

that his wife (spend) ______________________ the night with another man. Ptolemy then (threaten) ______________________ Caesar with revenge. In retaliation, Caesar (order) ______________________ Ptolemy's death. By the time Cleopatra and Caesar sailed for Rome, some guards (kill) ______________________ Ptolemy.

6. I (learn) ______________________ a lot about ancient Egypt since my course began. By the time we have our test tomorrow, I (study) ______________________ for about twenty hours!

Life Lessons

Work with a partner. Read the next three sentences out loud, taking turns completing them. Try to speak without stopping, and then brainstorm to come up with as many ideas as possible for the three scenarios.

1. By the time I entered primary school, I had learned …
2. By the time I finished high school, I had learned …
3. By the time I finish college, I will have learned …

EXAMPLE: By the time I entered primary school, I had learned to tie my shoes. I had also learned to share. I had not yet learned to be a good loser.

When you finish, write a paragraph about your partner based on his or her responses to one of the scenarios.

UNIT 5 Adjectives and Adverbs

Preview

MEN AND WOMEN

The Implicit Association Test* assumes that people make connections between familiar pairs of ideas. For example, if we hear the name "Amanda," we automatically associate it with a woman.

PART A

Try the next test. Be spontaneous. Don't spend too much time thinking about your choice. Just put a check mark in either the right or the left column.

Female		Male
______	emotional	______
______	a good cook	______
______	a strict parent	______
______	a fun parent	______
______	likes to shop	______
______	a good driver	______
______	aggressive	______
______	worries about appearance	______
______	nags and complains	______
______	supports family financially	______
______	peaceful	______

PART B

Discuss gender stereotypes, and then write a paragraph about the perceived differences between men and women.

* The Implicit Association Test was developed by Anthony G. Greenwald, Mahzarin Banaji, Brian Nosek, and other social psychology researchers.

Adjectives and Adverbs: Forms and Usage

Adjectives describe nouns (people, places, and things) and pronouns (words that replace nouns). They add information explaining how many, what kind, or which one. They can appear before nouns or after linking verbs such as *be*, *look*, *appear*, and *seem*.

Before a noun: She is an **intelligent** and **beautiful** woman.

After a linking verb: He seems **serious**.

Adverbs are words (or groups of words) that add information to verbs, adjectives, and other adverbs. Most adverbs end in *–ly*, but there are some exceptions, such as *fast*, *often*, and *hard*.

He works **quickly**.

COMPARATIVE AND SUPERLATIVE FORMS OF ADJECTIVES AND ADVERBS

	ADJECTIVE OR ADVERB	COMPARATIVE	SUPERLATIVE
A. Add *–er* or *–est* to one-syllable adjectives.	short fast	short**er** than fast**er** than	the short**est** the fast**est**
When an adjective ends in a consonant-vowel-consonant, double the last letter.	hot	hot**ter** than	the hot**test**
B. In two-syllable adjectives ending in a consonant + *–y*, change the *–y* to *–i* and add *–er* (comparative form) or *–est* (superlative form).	easy funny	eas**ier** than funn**ier** than	the eas**iest** the funn**iest**
C. Add *more* (comparative form) or *most* (superlative form) to adjectives of two or more syllables and to compound adjectives.	modern well-liked	**more** modern than **more** well-liked than	the **most** modern the **most** well-liked
D. Add *more* (comparative form) or *most* (superlative form) to adverbs ending in *–ly*.	easily quickly	**more** easily than **more** quickly than	the **most** easily the **most** quickly
E. Some adjectives and adverbs have special comparative and superlative forms.	good / well bad / badly much / many little (a small amount) far	**better** than **worse** than **more** than **less** than **farther** / **further*** than	the **best** the **worst** the **most** the **least** the **farthest** / the **furthest***

* *Farther* indicates a physical distance. *Further* means "additional" and *furthest* means "to the greatest degree." For example: I need **further** information before I can make a decision.

EQUALITY: *AS ... AS / THE SAME AS*

Both as ... as and *the same* as express equality.

The thief is **as old as** my father.

He ran away **as fast as** he could.

That cellphone is **the same colour as** mine.

Sometimes one object is not as "equal" as another.

Knives are **not as dangerous as** guns.

Practice

EXERCISE 1 **COMPARATIVE AND SUPERLATIVE FORMS OF ADJECTIVES**

Write either the comparative or superlative forms of the adjectives in parentheses. Remember to also write *than* or *the*.

EXAMPLE: One of (old) the oldest crime movies is about John Dillinger.

1. Many movies make criminals' lives appear (exciting) ____________ they really are. In movies, the criminals are (rich) ____________ ordinary people. Their houses and cars are (good) ____________ those of ordinary people. They have (good) ____________ lives of all because they can work whenever they want and buy whatever they desire. But in the real world, a life in crime is (difficult) ____________ life possible.
2. First, real-world criminals feel (guilty) ____________ ordinary people. Their lives are (bad) ____________ the lives of honest citizens. For instance, "Tim" sold cocaine in 2005, and one of his customers died. In an interview, Tim said, "My client had become a close friend. The day he died was (bad) ____________ day of my life! I could no longer pretend that my work was not hurting anyone."
3. Also, it is not always easy to leave a life of crime. In most criminal syndicates, members must commit for life. Leaving a criminal gang is (dangerous) ____________ leaving any other job. Honest citizens are (lucky) ____________ criminals. Definitely, an honest life is (good) ____________ a life of crime.

TIP

Than or *Then*?

In comparisons, use ***than***. Do not use ***then***, which means "next" or "after that."

The US has more prisons **than** ~~then~~ Canada does.

TWO-PART COMPARATIVES

Usually, you would use *the* in superlative rather than comparative forms. However, there are some two-part comparatives that require *the*. In these expressions, the second part is the result of the first part.

action / result

The more you exercise, **the better** you will feel.

EXERCISE 2 **IDENTIFY ERRORS**

Underline and correct twelve errors involving comparative forms of adjectives, including incorrect spelling.

strangest
EXAMPLE: That is the most strange information that I have ever heard.

1. The more greedier people are, the greatest the chance that they will commit a crime. Some individuals turn to crime because they want to be richest than before. They think that the most they spend, the happiest they will be. However, money seldom makes people feel best. In fact, when sociologists examined the most wealthiest Canadians, they discovered that their lives weren't better than the lives of their peers.

2. Generally, humans have a happiness set point. Often, after they gain a lot of money, they briefly feel more better. But after a couple of months, they return to their set point. Thus, they find new things to complain about, and sometimes their lives become worst than before. In a study, the extremely rich had higher drug-abuse rates then others. Extreme wealth may be the less important component of a person's happiness. In fact, the true indicator of happiness is personal relationships. The most close relationships someone has, the better he or she will feel.

SPELLING OF ADVERBS

When a word ends in *–l*, form the adverb by adding *–ly*.

The team of historians worked **carefully**.

When a two-syllable word ends in *–y*, form the adverb by changing the *–y* to *–i* and adding *–ly*.

They worked together **happily**.

TIP

Irregular Adverbs

Some adverbs such as *often* never end in *–ly*.

EXERCISE 3 **ADVERBS**

Decide if each of the following sentences requires an adjective or an adverb. Then add *–ly* if necessary. If no *–ly* is required, put an *X* instead.

EXAMPLE: The robber acted *quick*ly.

1. Ken Leishman was *responsible*_____ for a series of robberies in the 1950s and 1960s. He and his accomplices had to work very *quick*_____. In 1966, Leishman masterminded "the great gold heist," the largest theft of gold in Canadian history. After that crime, Leishman was *often*_____ referred to as the "Flying Bandit."

2. Leishman thought *serious*_____ about the gold theft while he was in prison for an earlier crime. He came up with an *extreme*_____ risky plan. After he got out, he was *cautious*_____, and he found accomplices to help do the crime. First, he *careful*_____ stencilled fake Air Canada logos on coveralls. He waited *patient*_____ until a clerk left an Air Canada desk, and then he stole some waybills, which are documents that give shipping instructions. His accomplices posed as airport security and, using a fake waybill, they *casual*_____ picked up the load of gold at the airport. The plan was *successful*_____.

3. Leishman was eventually imprisoned for the heist. He *successful*_____ escaped from prison and stole an airplane. Authorities caught him and then released him again. In 1975, he moved to a *peaceful*_____ town called Red Lake, Ontario. He lived there *quiet*_____ for four years. Later, in 1979, a plane he was flying *mysterious*_____ disappeared, reinforcing the myth of the "Flying Bandit." He was *official*_____ declared dead in 1980.

PLACEMENT OF FREQUENCY ADVERBS

Frequency adverbs—words such as *always*, *often*, *sometimes*, *usually*, and *ever*—indicate how often someone performs an action or how frequently an event occurs.

Place frequency adverbs before regular present and past tense verbs.

Police officers **sometimes** work at night.

Place frequency adverbs after the verb *be*.

The officer is **often** very busy.

Place frequency adverbs after auxiliary verbs.

She has **never** used her gun.

Real Versus *Really*

Real is an adjective that means "genuine" or "not fake."

He bought his girlfriend a **real** diamond.

Really is an adverb that means "in reality" or "actually." *Really* also expresses the degree to which something is true. **Note:** Never put *very* before a verb.

They worked **really** hard on the song. They ~~very~~ **really** wanted attention.

Ensure that you always modify a verb using an adverb.

The protestors yelled ~~real loud~~ **really loudly** during the riot.

EXERCISE 4 **IDENTIFY ERRORS**

Underline and correct ten errors involving adjective and adverb forms and word order.

EXAMPLE: Newspapers and magazines contain often (often contain) articles about corruption.

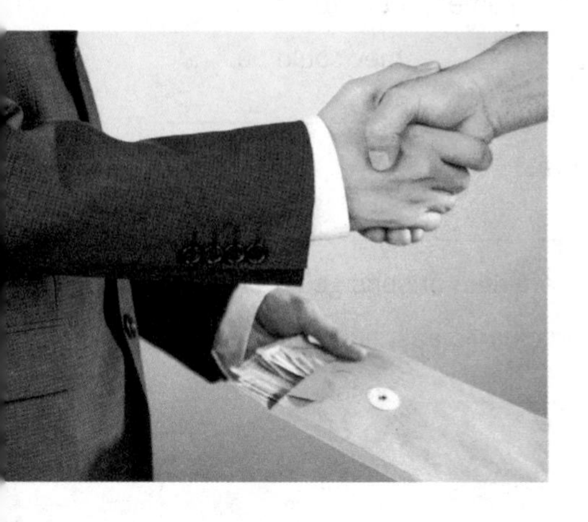

1. Most cities have political corruption. Mayors must carefuly deal with contractors for public works. Certain companies receive often the most building contracts. They act real suspiciously. Canadians, for instance, hear often about corruption in the construction industry, and they very want the government to take action. Politicians do not act quick enough when there are allegations of corruption.

2. Citizens often are skeptical about the political system. They believe usually that all politicians are dishonest. Perhaps governments will eventualy take action to stop corruption. I very hope so.

As ... As

Remember to use *as ... as* when two items have equal value.

Brad is **as** guilty ~~than~~ **as** his brother.

EXERCISE 5 ADJECTIVES AND ADVERBS

Complete each sentence with the correct form of the word in parentheses. You may need to change an adjective to an adverb. You may also need to supply the following words: *than* or *as ... as*.

EXAMPLE: The judge speaks (loud) more loudly than the lawyer.

1. Countries have different legal systems and sentencing guidelines. For example, in the US, sentences are (strict) ______________________ they are in Canada. Canadian prisoners usually get out of jail (quick) ______________________ ______________________ American prisoners. The Canadian system is not the same as the American system; it's not (harsh) ______________________ ______________________ the US system.

2. Certain prison guards attempt to be (nice) ______________________ to the criminals in their care than others do. Some guards treat prisoners (harsh) ______________________ others do. Certainly, guards earn (much money) ______________________ people in many other professions. Sometimes, they are not (compassionate) ______________________ they could be. Perhaps they should receive (good training) ______________________ ______________________ they currently receive.
3. Canadian prisoners are (lucky) ______________________ the prisoners of many other countries. Canadian prisons generally meet international standards of safety and cleanliness, and prisoners are treated (humane) ______________________ prisoners in many other countries.

GOOD/WELL AND BAD/BADLY

Good is an adjective, and ***well*** is an adverb.

Adjective: They had a very **good** relationship.
Adverb: They communicated really **well**.

Exception: Use *well* to describe a person's health.

She is not **well**. She has the flu.

Bad is an adjective, and ***badly*** is an adverb.

Adjective: Yoko was not a **bad** singer.
Adverb: However, some critics reacted **badly** to her work.

EXERCISE 6 ***GOOD, WELL, BAD, AND BADLY***

Underline the appropriate adjectives or adverbs in parentheses.

EXAMPLE: Some journalists write really (good / well).

When a major crime happens, the criminal (regular / regularly) receives more attention than the victim. In fact, some people commit crimes because they crave fame (bad / badly). They don't behave (good / well), yet they get a lot of attention. For example, the culprits in school shootings become (good / well) -known celebrities. The victims, who were (good / well) people, aren't remembered very (good / well). Perhaps the members of the media (bad / badly) need to change their focus. When a shooter opens fire on innocent people, his or her name should not be publicized. Criminals should not receive the attention that they want so (bad / badly). Perhaps (good / well) behaviour should be rewarded more than (bad / badly) behaviour.

FEWER* VERSUS *LESS

When you are comparing count nouns, use ***fewer*** or ***the fewest***. When you are comparing noncount nouns, use ***less*** or ***the least***. (For more information about noncount nouns, see Unit 8, page 77.)

Count noun:	Blainville has **the fewest criminals** in Quebec.
Noncount noun:	I have **less time** than you do.

Note: Use *less* and *the least* when another adjective appears before the noun.

Rene had **the least believable alibi**.

TIP

Adjective or Noun?

A noun may act like an adjective when it modifies another noun. Remember that adjectives are singular.

The shirt costs fifty **dollars**. (*Dollars* is a noun.)	It is a fifty-**dollar** shirt. (*Dollar* acts as an adjective and modifies *shirt*.)

EXERCISE 7 **IDENTIFY ERRORS**

Underline and correct errors involving adjectives or adverbs. Write *C* next to correct sentences.

EXAMPLE: He is a person simples. (correction: simple person)

1. A prison is a multi-million-dollars building.

→

2. The average prisoner is a thirty-three-years-old man.
3. Canada incarcerates less people than many other countries do.
4. The average sentence for armed robbery is seven years-and-a-half.
5. Regina is the less safe city in Canada.
6. Crime movies are less realistic than other types of movies.
7. Children are influenced more easier than adults are.
8. Sometimes children very hope to become criminals.
9. After Rick committed a crime, he escaped as quickly than he could, but the police caught him.
10. Rick's prison cell has no paper toilet.
11. A typical school has fewer rules than a prison does.
12. Mexico has the bigger crime problem in North America.
13. Canadians have less guns than Americans do.
14. Which country has the least problems?
15. Most countries have real big problems with drug gangs.

UNIT Review

Complete the following exercise. If you don't know an answer, go back and review the appropriate section.

Underline and correct the errors in the sentences below.

1. If you complain, it will make things worst than before. ____________
2. Carol has as much money than I do. ____________
3. Bill is a more better businessman than Donald. ____________
4. The harder you work, the worst you will feel. ____________
5. Alex does the less amount of work of anyone that I know. ____________
6. Alex sings real good. ____________
7. He feels bad about his situation. ____________
8. the guards work often overtime. ____________

My eLab

Need more practice? Visit My eLab and try more grammar exercises.

Final Review

PART A

Write the correct comparative or superlative form of each word in parentheses. In some cases, you may need to change an adjective to an adverb. You may also need to add *the* or *than*. Do not use *as ... as*.

EXAMPLE: A sentencing circle is (good) better than a regular courtroom.

1. In past centuries, shaming penalties were very common. Judges ordered shaming penalties much (frequent) ______________________ they do today. One of (bad) ______________________ penalties involved the pillory. The wooden structure could lock a person's hands and head in place. The goal was to publicly humiliate the offender. Sometimes, even (nice) ______________________ citizens in town would spit on the criminal. In addition, in the past, police officers were (powerful) ______________________ they are today. They could arrest people (easy) ______________________ they can today. Nowadays, there are many protections for citizens.

2. Today, shaming penalties are rare, but they are coming back in fashion. For example, a judge in Wisconsin orders shoplifters to stand in front of the stores they robbed, holding a sign that reads, "I am a shoplifter." One shoplifter said the shaming was (bad) ______________________ jail. "All of my neighbours saw me. It was (sad) ______________________ day of my life," said Reena King.

3. Near Boston, when a ferry owner poured pollutants directly into the ocean, a passenger called the police. These days, ocean polluting is treated (severe) ______________________ it was in the past. In court, the judge ordered the ferry owner to put a full-page ad in a Boston newspaper, reading, "Our company has discharged human waste into coastal waters." The ferry owner said that paying a fine is (easy) ______________________ facing public humiliation. For companies, bad publicity is (effective) ______________________ type of punishment.

4. Some judges say that the shaming system works. Nowadays, people change their behaviour (quick) ______________________ they did in the past

because they realize they might face public humiliation. Many judges believe that public shaming is (good) ______________________________ penalty of all.

PART B

Underline and correct the errors involving adjectives or adverbs. Write *C* beside any sentence that is correct.

EXAMPLE: The thief was a <u>real</u> greedy man. (really)

5. Sam Rice did his most biggest crime in 2011.

6. The more Sam stole, the better he felt.

7. He believed that he was the less likely criminal in the city to get arrested.

8. Sam thought that he could blend in with the crowds really good.

9. But one day, he was not as careful as his accomplice was.

10. In the end, his criminal skills were not as good than he thought, and he ended up in prison.

11. These days, he has less ideas about stealing than he did in the past.

12. Sam wants to change his life, and he doesn't want to behave bad anymore.

Crime and Consequences

Work with a partner, and discuss one of the following topics. Then write sentences that use the comparative form, the superlative form, and the equal (*as ... as*) form of adjectives and adverbs.

1. Should youths be judged less harshly than adults are for crimes? Why or why not?
2. What are the best and worst punishments for prisoners?
3. Who gets more attention when a major crime happens: the criminal or the victim? Why?
4. Who commits more crime: males or females? Discuss why one gender is more likely to commit criminal acts.

UNIT 6

Modal Auxiliaries

Preview

LETTERS OF ADVICE

Work with a partner and read the following e-mails. Discuss what each letter writer should do. Then compose letters of advice to the writers.

My partner is an alcoholic. She promised to stop drinking when we got married, and I believed her. Now we've been married for a month, and she still drinks a lot of wine every day. About three times a week, she comes to bed completely drunk. Should I have married her? What should I have done when I learned that she is an alcoholic?

Anonymous

A few months ago, I discovered that my fourteen-year-old son was a hacker. After I got suspicious and checked his computer, I found a page showing people's credit card numbers and passwords. He promised to stop hacking, but he still seems to have a lot of money and doesn't tell me where it is from. I don't like to punish him, but I'm worried that he'll get into trouble. What mistakes have I made? What should I do now?

Sofia

Modal Auxiliaries: Forms and Usage

COMMON MODAL AUXILIARIES

FUNCTION	MODAL	EXAMPLE	PAST FORM
ability	**can**	I **can climb** mountains.	**could climb**
polite request (question form)	**may** **would** **could** **can**	**May** I **help** you? (formal) **Would** you **like** some coffee? **Could** you **open** the door? **Can** I **help** you? (informal)	
advice* opinion	**should** **ought to**	She **should see** a lawyer. The lawyer **ought to meet** her.	**should have seen** **ought to have met**
obligation	**must** **have to****	Now, the baby **must sleep.** Now, she **has to sleep.**	**had to sleep** (past form of both *must* and *have to*)
probability	**must**	Chantal **must be** tired.	**must have been**
possibility	**could** **might** **may**	The clerk **could help** you. I **might take** the job. Ann **may need** them.	**could have helped** **might have taken** **may have needed**
conditional action desire / preference past habit	**would** **would like** **would rather**	If I had time, I **would visit** her. (expresses a wish) I **would like** some coffee. I **would rather be** happy than rich. In my youth, I **would drive** for hours.	**would have visited** **would have liked** **would rather have been**

* You can use the form ***had better*** to indicate a strong recommendation.

You **had better hurry** or you'll miss the bus.

** Although *have to* is not a modal auxiliary, it is included here because it functions like a modal and has the same meaning as *must*. Its third-person-singular form is *has to*. For the past, use *had to*, and for the future, use *will have to*.

Practice

EXERCISE 1 **MIXED MODALS**

Insert the appropriate modals in the blanks. The function of each modal is indicated in parentheses. In some cases, more than one answer is possible.

EXAMPLE: We (*advice:* leave) <u>should leave</u> now. It's getting late.

1. According to the BBC News, Britain is a "surveillance society." England has one security camera for every thirty people. Citizens (*advice:* drive, not) ______________________ over the speed limit because speed cameras are on highways. Police (*ability:* give) ______________________ really large fines

to people who speed. Cameras on telephone poles and storefronts (*possibility:* film) ______________________ people who commit crimes.

2. Simon Davies, of the watchdog group Privacy International, believes he (*obligation:* speak) ______________________ about Britain's increasing use of closed-circuit cameras. He points out that Britain has more surveillance cameras than China does. England (*possibility:* become) ______________________ ______________________ a police state. According to Davies, "In the past, we (*past ability:* walk) ______________________ on public streets without being filmed. Today, we (*obligation:* be) ______________________ careful because we are all under surveillance." Davies thinks people (*advice:* protest) ______________________ about the issue.

MUST NOT VERSUS *DON'T HAVE TO*

Both *must* and *have to* indicate that something is necessary. However, the meanings are different in the negative form.

Must not means something is not permitted.

You **must not touch** that bomb. It is too dangerous!

Don't have to means there is no obligation, but you can do it if you want.

You **don't have to stay** here. You can leave.

EXERCISE 2 *MUST NOT* OR *DON'T HAVE TO*

Fill in the blanks with the negative form of either *must* or *have to*.

EXAMPLE: The children <u>must not</u> touch the dog. He is very fierce.

1. In Canada, you ______________________ carry a baby on your lap while driving. It is illegal.
2. In England, you ______________________ drive on the right side of the road. The traffic laws are different, and everyone must drive on the left side of the road.
3. In English pubs, you ______________________ tip the bartender. It isn't expected.
4. England has strict gun-control laws. You ______________________ bring a firearm into the country. It is illegal.
5. Marley ______________________ stay at a hotel. If he wants, he can stay with us.

PAST FORMS OF *MUST*

Must can indicate an obligation, but it can also mean that something is probable.

When *must* means "it is necessary," the past form is *had to.*

She **must leave** now. Yesterday, she **had to leave**.

When *must* means "it is probable," the past form is *must have* + the past participle.

He **must be** tired. Yesterday, he **must have been** tired.

EXERCISE 3 **PAST FORMS OF *MUST***

Read the first sentence in each pair, and decide if *must* indicates a probability (*P*) or an obligation (*O*). Then complete the second sentence with the correct past form of *must* (*must* or *have to*).

EXAMPLE: There **must be** a problem with the engine. P

Past form: Yesterday, there must have been a problem with the engine.

1. Layla's new smart phone **must cost** a lot. ____

   Past form: Layla's old cellphone ________________ a lot.

2. According to her contract, Layla **must pay** for Internet access on her phone. ____

   Past form: Last year, Layla ________________ for Internet access on her phone.

3. Her phone is too large for her pocket, so she **must carry** it in her purse. ____

   Past form: Her old phone was also large, so she ________________ it in her purse.

4. She lost her new phone. She **must be** upset. ____

   Past form: Last year, she lost her phone. She ________________ upset.

5. Layla fell and cut her hand, so she **must get** stitches. ____

   Past form: Last month, she cut her foot, and she ________________ stitches.

PAST FORMS OF *SHOULD*, *COULD*, AND *WOULD*

To form the past tense of modals such as *should*, *could*, and *would*, add *have* + the past participle.

Before Rosalie and Mark went to Panama, they **should have learned** a few words in Spanish. They **could have communicated** with the locals, and they **would have had** a better time.

EXERCISE 4 PRESENT AND PAST MODALS

Insert the appropriate modals in the blanks. In some cases, there may be more than one answer.

EXAMPLE: When he was a child, he (can, write) could write computer code.

1. Michael Calce was born in 1985 in Montreal. After his parents divorced, he (have to, go) ______________ back and forth from his mother's house to his father's downtown condo. When he was six years old, his father gave him a computer. By the time he was a teenager, Michael (can, hack) ______________ into very complex computer systems. Of course, he (must, use) ______________ an alias when he hacked. In 2000, he chose the name MafiaBoy. At that time, he (should, know) ______________ that the name was provocative.

2. At the age of fifteen, Calce carried out one of the first major computer hacks in the world. In 2000, companies such as CNN, Yahoo, Amazon, and Dell (have to, pay) ______________ a lot of money to repair the damage caused by Calce. They realized that they (should, prepare) ______________ for cyber attacks at that time. They (must, be) ______________ shocked that the perpetrator was a fifteen-year-old Canadian. From 2001 to 2005, Calce's actions (may, prompt) ______________ many companies to improve their security systems.

3. Today, companies (can, spend) ______________ millions of dollars making sure their computer systems are secure. Still, the possibility exists that another teenager (might, infiltrate) ______________ the website or data of a major corporation. Back when I was in university, I probably (should, study) ______________ computer science. Then I (would, find) ______________ a better job when I graduated in 2006.

QUESTION FORMS

In question forms, move the modal auxiliary before the subject.

They **can** dance well.	**Can** they dance well?
He **should** have helped.	**Should** he have helped?

Exception: *Have to*

Remember that *have to* is actually a regular verb, so you need to add *do*, *does*, or *did* to question forms.

Bruno **has to** work late.	**Does** Bruno **have to** work late?

EXERCISE 5 QUESTIONS WITH MODALS

Write questions for the sentences below. The answers to the questions are in bold.

EXAMPLE: We should go **to Toronto** next summer.
Where should we go next summer?

1. **Yes**, we can participate in the flash mob.

 ____

2. We should bring **pillows**.

 ____

3. **International Pillow Fight Day** might occur in Montreal.

 ____

4. News about this event can spread **through social networking sites**.

 ____

5. **Last year's Toronto event** must have been fun.

 ____

6. Chantal had to leave early **because she didn't have a pillow with her.**

 ____

7. She should have brought **a pillow** to the flash-mob event.

 ____

8. This year's event could last **about two hours**.

 ____

NEVER WRITE *SHOULD OF*, *SHOULDA*, OR *GOTTA*

Should of* and *Shoulda

In spoken English, it sounds as if people are saying "should of" or "shoulda." These are non-standard forms, and you should avoid using them. Instead, for the past forms of *should*, *could*, and *would*, always include *have* + the past participle.

When Calce hacked computers, he ~~shoulda~~ **should have** known it was dangerous. Maybe his parents ~~would of~~ **would have** taken action.

Gotta

Similarly, *gotta* is not a standard word and should never be written. It is an incorrect contraction of *got* and *to*. In formal English, it is preferable to write and say *have to*, as in, "I have to leave." In informal English, you can also say, "I've got to leave."

I ~~gotta~~ **have to** buy a new laptop because mine stopped working.

EXERCISE 6 **IDENTIFY MODAL ERRORS**

Underline and correct ten errors involving modal forms.

EXAMPLE: Reena <u>shoulda</u> (should have) changed her password.

1. Last month, Reena took a short break from work. She coulda stayed home, but instead her boyfriend invited her to his parents' country house. One Tuesday morning, they set out on their trip. Reena was texting when she drove into a fence. Luckily, they weren't hurt, but they could of had serious injuries. She should have pull over to the side of the road before writing a text message.

2. Reena had to stayed in contact with her workplace, so she brought along her laptop. One morning, she went to buy food. The grocery store was crowded, so she can't finish her shopping quickly and she spent about two hours in the store. While she was shopping, Reena's boyfriend used her computer. Reena shouldn't of told him the password. He went online and read Reena's e-mails and chat logs. He definitely would seen comments that she had made about him. When Reena realized what he had done, she shoulda yelled at him, but she didn't want to embarrass him in front of his parents. Reena's boyfriend claims that anyone woulda done what he did. Reena disagrees and argues that people gotta respect each other's privacy. Who do you agree with?

UNIT Review

Complete the following exercises. If you don't know an answer, go back and review the appropriate section.

1. Write the past form of each modal verb in bold.
   a) Amber **must go** home. ____________
   b) She **can write** computer programs. ____________
   c) He **should change** his password. ____________
   d) We **have to leave**. ____________

→

2. Underline and correct the errors involving modal forms in the following sentences.

EXAMPLE: I <u>coulda</u> helped you yesterday. could have

a) You should've went to Calgary. ______

b) I really gotta find a better job. ______

c) When I was a child, I can ran really fast. ______

d) He must of been with his father yesterday. ______

Final Review

Underline and correct fifteen errors involving modal forms, including the use of *gotta*.

EXAMPLE: Maybe Sabu <u>coulda</u> saved himself. (could have)

1. I gotta tell you about some hackers associated with the Anonymous group. In 2011, a small group of hackers known as LulzSec decided that they would taking down the CIA website. They also decided to hack the FBI. They were confident that nobody can find out who they were. But those hackers shouldn't had been so cocky. By May 2011, FBI agents knew that they had to found LulzSec.

2. On June 7, 2011, two FBI agents put on their bulletproof vests and went to a housing complex in New York's Lower East Side. That day was sweltering, so the agents probably woulda been hot and sweaty. One agent knocked on the steel door at the home of Hector Xavier Monsegur, a twenty-eight-year-old unemployed father of two. Monsegur, who used the online name Sabu, can't believe it when he saw the agents. He knew that he gotta do something to save himself. In a plea bargain, Sabu agreed to work undercover and unmask

his co-hackers. Of course, he must of felt really guilty, but he didn't want to lose his children and spend his life in prison.

3. In March 2012, two British citizens were arrested for being part of the group of hackers. Ryan Ackroyd, a twenty-five-year-old man, pretended to be a teen girl, Kayla, when he was online. He shoulda been more suspicious of Sabu. A few days later, Jake Davis, an eighteen-year-old hacker who used the name Topiary, was also arrested. He would of been shocked when the police turned up at his door. Finally, in July 2012, TFlow, a sixteen-year-old male from London, was caught. None of them can escaped, and they were sent to jail. The larger Anonymous hacker community must of felt upset in 2012.

4. These days, Governments know that they gotta do something about computer hacking. Many believe that the four LulzSec hackers should not attacked government and corporate websites and that their arrest was justified. Others support the hackers. Of course, since then, other hackers have filled the void left by the arrests.

Regrets

Work with a partner and imagine the regrets that people in the following two situations feel. Explain what they could have done and should (or should not) have done. Then, on a piece of paper, write at least three sentences about each person's regrets. Give reasons for each statement.

SITUATION A

Taylor Greene, a financial advisor, convinced his friends and family members to unknowingly invest in fake companies. Greene spent the money and used new investors' money to pay older investors. Eventually, his scheme was discovered.

SITUATION B

During his six-year hacking career, Hector Xavier Monsegur started a group similar to Anonymous and he destroyed the reputations of many people. The FBI arrested him and convinced him to work undercover and expose other hackers. He agreed.

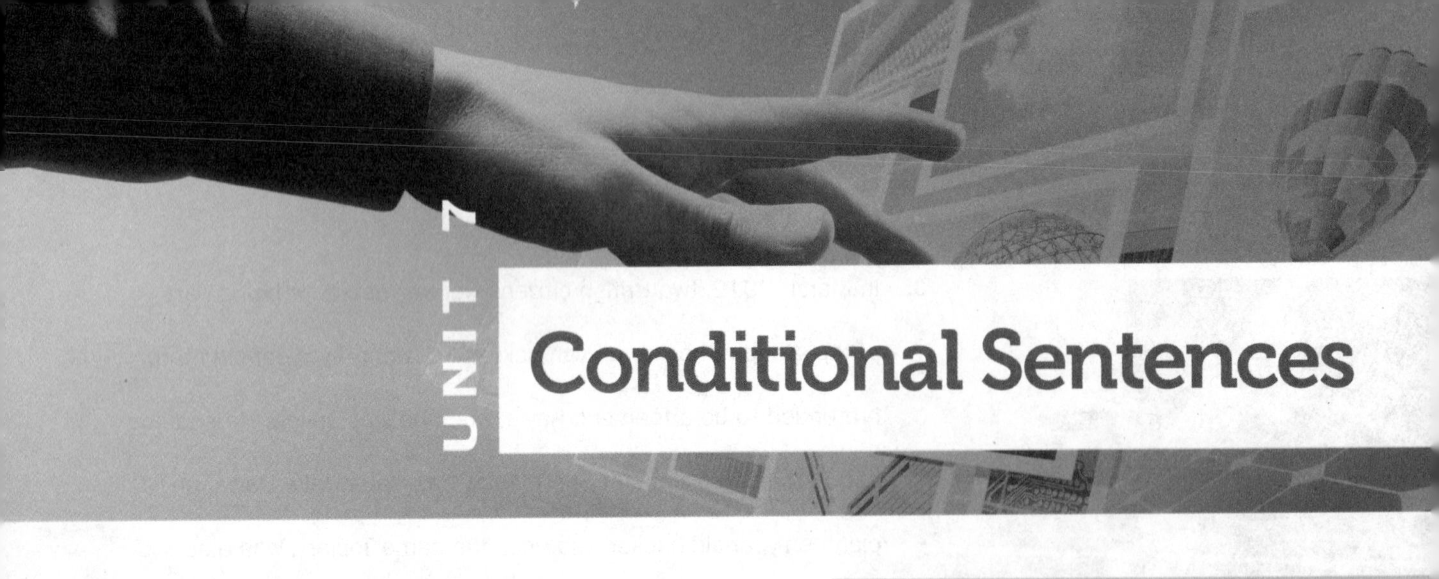

Conditional Sentences

Preview

NON-STOP TALKING

Work with a partner or a small team and, one person at a time, speak non-stop about topic A, below. When the teacher flicks the light switch, change speakers. Repeat until all students have spoken, and then begin the exercise again, this time, speaking non-stop about topic B.

A. IF I COULD LIVE FOR 200 YEARS

Scientists are working hard to increase life expectancy. If you knew that you could live to be 200, how would your life change?

B. IF I HAD LIVED IN THE 1800s

Imagine what your life would have been like if you had lived in the 1800s. How would your life have been different?

Conditional Sentences: Forms and Usage

In conditional sentences, there are conditions and results. These types of sentences usually contain two clauses. The **main clause** depends on the condition set in the ***if* clause**. There are three conditional forms.

TYPES OF CONDITIONAL SENTENCES

1. **Possible Present or Future**
   Use this form when the condition is true or very possible.

Condition (*if* clause)	Result
If + present tense ⟶	present or future tense
If you **think** about it, (This present situation is true.)	life **is** fantastic.
If you **quit** your job, (This future situation is possible.)	you **won't be able to pay** the rent.

2. **Unlikely Present**
   Use this form when the condition is not likely and probably will not happen.

Condition (*if* clause)	Result
If + past tense ⟶	*would* (expresses a condition) *could* (expresses a possibility)

If I **won** money in a lottery, **I would build** a house.
(This condition is unlikely.)

If Eva **knew** how to speak Greek, she **could take** the job in Athens.

When the *if* clause contains *be*, always use *were*, even when the subject is *I*, *he*, *she*, or *it*. In informal speech, you may hear "was" in the *if* clause.

If I **were** rich, I **would buy** a new car.
If my sister **were** rich, she **would spend** a lot on clothing.

3. **Impossible Past**

Use this form when the condition cannot happen because the event is over.

Condition (*if* clause)		**Result**
If + past perfect tense	→	*would have* + past participle *could have* + past participle

If my grandfather **had won** money, he **would have given** it away.
If you **had told** me about the problem, I **could have stopped** the project.

MAKING A WISH

Wish about the Present

You make a wish when you want things to be different. When you **wish about a present situation**, use the past tense. When you **wish to change** a habit, use *would* or *could*.

I **wish** I **had** a great singing voice. (I can't sing, but I would like to.)
I **wish** you **would stop** smoking. (I wish you would change a habit.)

Wish about the Past

When you **wish you could change a past situation**, use the past perfect tense.

Leo **wishes** that he **had told** the truth to his wife.

Practice

EXERCISE 1 TYPES OF CONDITIONAL SENTENCES

Identify the types of conditional sentences. Write *A* (possible present or future), *B* (unlikely present), or *C* (impossible past) in the spaces provided.

EXAMPLE: If he gets the job, he will be really happy. A

1. If Jacob were older, he would apply for the job. _____
2. If you want to learn about architecture, Jacob will teach you. _____
3. If he had studied more, perhaps he would have passed all of his courses. _____
4. Architecture is fascinating if you learn to appreciate it. _____
5. He would design a new arena if the city hired him. _____
6. If he had gone into the family business, he would have felt unfulfilled. _____

EXERCISE 2 PRESENT AND PAST CONDITIONAL FORMS

Choose the correct form of each verb. Decide if the situation is possible or unlikely. Then use the possible present or future conditional form or the unlikely present conditional form.

EXAMPLE: If you play the scales every day, you (improve) will improve a lot.

1. James McCann has an unbelievable memory. If he looks at an image for about ten seconds, he (remember) ____________________ everything about it. This kind of memory is known as eidetic memory. If McCann (drive) ____________________ down my street today, he would be able to detail every house, driveway, and hedge along the whole street. However, he probably won't visit my street.
2. McCann's memory is a fascinating subject for a psychology professor at his university. If the university (pay) ____________________ McCann, he will let himself be tested for the sake of science. However, if the university (help, not) ____________________ financially, he will probably not consent to the study. McCann lives in Brisbane, Australia. If he (live) ____________________ in Canada, he probably (enjoy, not) ____________________ the climate. Brisbane has a very nice climate.

EXERCISE 3 IMPOSSIBLE PAST CONDITIONAL FORMS

Complete the following sentences using the impossible past conditional form of the verbs in parentheses.

EXAMPLE: If the police (conduct) had conducted an investigation, they would have solved the case.

1. Is hacking ethical? Mark Ward, in *A Brief History of Hacking*, says that in the past "hackers were benign creatures." A "hack" was "an inspired solution to a problem." If you (live) ____________________ in the 1980s, you (admire) ____________________ hackers. Most early hackers just wanted to find the flaws in computer systems. Some of them played silly pranks. For instance, Steve Jobs hacked into telephone systems to make free phone calls. Perhaps if the police (arrest) ____________________ Jobs back in the 1980s, he (create, not) ____________________ Apple Computer.
2. Another early hacker went by the name Dark Dante. He took over the phone lines when radio shows had contests, and as a result won major prizes. For instance, in 1990, when a Los Angeles radio show announced that the 102nd

caller would win a prize, Dark Dante used his hacking skills to ensure that he was the 102nd caller, so he won a Porsche. If those radio stations (know) ______________ their phone lines were being hacked, they (change) ______________ their contest rules. After such exploits became well-known, new anti-hacking laws were introduced.

EXERCISE 4 **CONDITIONAL VERBS**

For the following sentences, write the correct conditional form of each verb in parentheses.

EXAMPLE: If he (live) <u>had lived</u> in an earlier era, Mark Zuckerberg would not have created Facebook.

Mark Zuckerberg

1. If you do research on the Internet, you (learn) ______________ a lot about Mark Zuckerberg. In 2002, the then-eighteen-year-old man wrote a computer program called Synapse. Bill Gates heard about Synapse. If Mark Zuckerberg (want) ______________ a job at Microsoft, he could have had one. Instead, he decided to stay at Harvard. For sure, if he (accept) ______________ the Microsoft job offer, his life (be) ______________ different. If he had left Harvard, he probably (think, never) ______________ about a college-based social networking site.

2. The following year, at Harvard, twins Cameron and Tyler Winklevoss asked Zuckerberg to help them write the programming code for a site called Harvard Connection. If Zuckerberg (refuse) ______________ to help the twins, he (save) ______________ himself a lot of problems. But Zuckerberg agreed to help them, and then he quickly abandoned the project. Instead, in his dorm room, Zuckerberg built his own social networking site. This early version of Facebook was an immediate hit. At the end of the year, Zuckerberg dropped out of Harvard to run his site. He made the right decision. If he (stay) ______________ at Harvard, it's likely that Facebook (be) ______________ less successful.

3. Back in 2003, if the Winklevoss twins (give) ______________ Zuckerberg a written contract, they (share) ______________ more fully in Facebook's profits. Today, the Winklevoss twins believe that Zuckerberg was unethical. But Zuckerberg argues that Facebook was original and was not similar to Harvard Connection. If I (be) ______________ →

Zuckerberg, maybe I would feel the same way. Unfortunately, I don't know how to build websites. But if I (know) ____________________ how to do it, I certainly (try) ____________________ to come up with a great idea for a website.

AVOIDING PROBLEMS WITH THE PAST CONDITIONAL

In **impossible past conditional** sentences, the writer expresses a wish that a past event had worked out differently. Avoid the following common errors.

Do not use *would have* or *could have* in the *if* clause. Use the past perfect tense instead.

had asked
If you ~~would have asked~~ me, I would have travelled with you.

Do not write *woulda / coulda* or *would of / could of*, as they are non-standard forms. When you use the past forms of *would* and *could*, always include *have* + the past participle.

have
If you had done your homework, you would ~~of~~ passed the course.

EXERCISE 5 IDENTIFY ERRORS

Underline and correct twelve errors involving conditional forms in the following sentences.

would have
EXAMPLE: If you had met Anna Chapman, you woulda liked her.

1. On a warm June day in 2010, Anna Chapman was sitting in a Manhattan coffee shop. If the shop would have had free Wi-Fi, the Facebook addict would have check her Facebook page. However, the shop didn't offer free Internet access. If you woulda seen Chapman that day, you woulda smiled. She looked like the girl next door, but the perky redhead was actually an undercover Russian spy.

Anna Chapman

2. Chapman's guest arrived. The good-looking man said he was working for the Russian consulate. In fact, he was an FBI agent. He offered Chapman a deal. She would earn a lot of money if she delivers a fake passport to another Russian spy. Perhaps if Chapman would have been more suspicious, she would have stayed out of trouble. But she agreed to do the transfer. If I was there, I would have warned her to be more careful. Soon after, Chapman and nine other Russian spies were arrested.

3. Normally, if someone betrays his or her nation, that person would go to prison. However, the US and Russia didn't want to damage their relationship. High-ranking politicians decided that they would make a deal if it is possible. In the end, America returned the ten spies to Russia and received four prisoners in exchange. If this deal had favoured the Russians, the US probably would not agree to it. It was actually better for the Americans. The four Americans in Russia had given extremely important information to Western nations before they were caught. The ten Russian spies, however, were "rank amateurs" according to the London newspaper the *Daily Mirror*. If Chapman wouldn't have been a spy, she could have stay in America. Instead, she can never return to North America.

EXERCISE 6 **WISHING AND CONDITIONAL FORMS**

Complete the sentences using the correct form of the verbs in parentheses. To review information about making a wish, see page 67.

EXAMPLE: I wish I (know) knew the answer now, but I don't.

1. Clay is always busy. He works part-time and attends law school. These days, he wishes that he (have) ________________ more time for a social life, but his studies are very demanding. He has a new girlfriend, and she is very needy. Clay wishes that she (call, not) ________________________ so often. Last year, Clay broke up with his previous girlfriend, Jaden. Now he wishes that he (leave, not) ________________________ her. He wishes that he (stay) ________________________ with Jaden, but it is too late. She has a new boyfriend.

2. Clay doesn't enjoy his university program. He has spoken with several lawyers who wish they (choose) ________________________ another field. They warned Clay that most jobs related to law are not very glamorous or well-paid. One lawyer named Marcus said, "I don't enjoy my job. I wish I (know) ________________________ about the long hours when I was still a student. I would never have become a lawyer."

3. Clay often wishes that he (take) ________________________ a computer-related program instead of switching to law after his undergraduate degree. He wishes that he (think) ________________________ more about his future.

THE DIFFERENCE BETWEEN *HOPE* AND *WISH*

Use ***hope*** when you want something to happen, but are not sure that it will (or did) happen.

I **hope** Joan's boyfriend **is** a nice guy. (I am not sure that he is nice.)
I **hope** that I **pass** this course. (I don't know if I will pass the course.)
I **hope** my brother **found** his car keys. (I don't know if he found them.)

Use ***wish*** when you want to alter a present or past situation. People usually wish for improbable or unlikely things. Keep in mind that changing a past situation is *impossible*).

I **wish** that I **had** more money. (I wish that I could change my present reality.)
I **wish** he **would stop** smoking. (I wish that he would change his bad habit.)
I **wish** I **had met** Jacob. (I wish that I could change a past event.)

TIP

Hope or Wish

To express a desire about a situation that was, is, or might be possible, use ***hope***. Don't use ***wish*** with the present tense.

hope
I ~~wish~~ I finish this project soon. I **wish** I had more time to work on it.

EXERCISE 7 ***HOPE OR WISH***

Fill in the blanks with *hope* or *wish*, as appropriate.

EXAMPLE: I hope the bank is still open.

1. I am looking for an apartment. I ________________ I can find a place that's close to school. I ________________ I could afford to live in a bigger apartment.
2. Next week, I have a job interview. I ________________ that I will be hired. I ________________ I had more experience to put on my CV, but I have only had one job. I ________________ I'm able to charm the interviewer. I have been preparing for days. I ________________ I knew someone at the company because that could help my chances.
3. My father is coming to visit tomorrow. I ________________ he has something to do while he's here. I ________________ I could spend more time with him, and I ________________ he understands that I don't mean to be rude, but I have a lot of studying to do.

EXERCISE 8 **IDENTIFY ERRORS**

Underline and correct eight errors involving conditional verb forms and the incorrect usage of *hope* or *wish*.

were
EXAMPLE: Many people wish that there is more sites like WikiLeaks.

1. In 2006, Julian Assange founded WikiLeaks. Then, in 2010, WikiLeaks published the content of a lot of sensitive diplomatic cables and documents. The documents embarrassed government officials in many nations. Those government workers probably wish that WikiLeaks kept the documents secret. For example, US politician Hillary Clinton wishes that people didn't read embarrassing comments about her.

2. In 2010, Bradley Manning, a US soldier, was arrested for supplying secret documents to WikiLeaks. Today, Manning is in prison, and he's serving a life sentence. He probably wishes that he didn't pass along those documents. He probably also wishes that he thought more about the consequences of his actions. Manning's supporters hope that he would be released from prison soon. Certainly, if he would have resisted the urge to send those documents to WikiLeaks, he would be a free man today.

3. I wish I knew about WikiLeaks when it was first launched. I think whistle-blower websites are fascinating. I wish that such sites always exist.

UNIT Review

Complete the following exercises. If you don't know an answer, go back and review the appropriate section.

1. For each sentence, write the verb *buy* in the correct tense form.
   a) I ______________________ it if I save enough money.
   b) I ______________________ it if I had a better job.
   c) I ______________________ it if I had known what a great deal it was.
2. Underline and correct the verb tense error in each sentence.
   a) If I would be younger, I would move to New York.

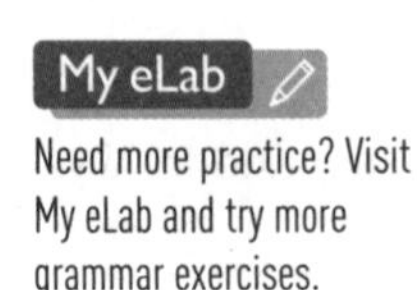

Need more practice? Visit My eLab and try more grammar exercises.

b) If the public would have known about Senator Klee's problems, they would have voted against him.

c) Soon Yi wishes that she has more money.

d) If Soon Yi were at the rally, she would have helped Senator Klee.

Final Review

PART A

Write the correct form of the verbs in parentheses.

EXAMPLE: If the police (conduct) had conducted an investigation, the case would have been solved.

1. In the early 2000s, the British tabloid *News of the World* hacked into the cellphones of celebrities. Journalists used the information they uncovered to write gossipy stories. The public was not very interested. Perhaps if people (show) ____________ ____________ more concern, the hacking (stop) ____________ sooner. Unfortunately, people expect celebrities to have no privacy. For instance, if somebody (listen) ____________ to actress Jennifer Lawrence's phone messages, nobody would worry about it. If a magazine published a celebrity's private phone messages, a lot of people (read) ____________ the article.

2. In 2011, everything changed for *News of the World*. A lawyer announced that nine years earlier, journalists had hired hackers to access the cellphone of a thirteen-year old murder victim, Milly Dowler, and that some of her voice-mail messages had been deleted after the hackers had listened to them. Journalists wrote that if *News of the World* hackers (leave) ____________ Dowler's phone alone, police (spend) ____________ more time on the case. Because her messages had been deleted, police and family members assumed that she was still alive. Perhaps if the phone hackers

(consider) ______________________ the family's feelings, they (act) ______________________ differently.

3. If *News of the World* employees had hacked into the phones of celebrities only, perhaps the publication (avoid) ______________________ closer scrutiny. But because they hacked into the phones of ordinary people, citizens were outraged. Rupert Murdoch had to shut down *News of the World* in the summer of 2011 because of the scandal. If the editors had acted responsibly, the newspaper (survive) ______________________.

PART B

Underline and correct five errors involving conditional forms of verbs.

4. I want to be a journalist. If I worked hard, I will succeed. Last year, I planned to enter a writing contest, but I didn't finish my essay in time. I wish I entered the contest because the prize was $1000. Maybe if I would have entered the contest, I would have won.

5. If one person owned all of Canada's newspapers, will there be a problem? In fact, most of Canada's media outlets are controlled by only a few companies. In 1990, over 17 percent of Canadian newspapers were independently owned. By 2005, that number had dropped to 1 percent. Maybe if Canada had had better anti-monopoly laws, that wouldn't of happened. Media consolidation can be dangerous because a few individuals can control what the public learns.

If ...

Discuss the following situations with a partner. Then, on a separate sheet of paper, create sentences explaining how you feel about each situation.

1. If you could have a special talent, what type of talent would you like to have?
2. If your parents had had a billion dollars, how would your childhood have been different?
3. Which celebrity do you wish you had met before he or she died? If you had met that person, what would you have said? (Examples: Mahatma Gandhi, Amy Winehouse, Napoleon, Pancho Villa, etc.)
4. What two things do you wish you had done in the past?

UNIT 8

Nouns, Determiners, and Pronouns

Preview

Work with a partner to identify and correct twelve mistakes in the following paragraph.

In 1989, Kalle Lasn and Bill Schmalz started a new medias foundation. At first, they had very few informations about the magazine market, but they forged ahead and produced a popular magazine and website. Today, much peoples with all type of lifestyles subscribe to *Adbusters*. In fact, it has more than ten thousands subscribers. Two years ago, my parents gave a subscription to the magazine to my brother and I. Many contributor to the magazine have created amusing spoofs ads. For example, last year, someone mocked a Joe Camel cigarette advertisement. The ad depicts "Joe Chemo" in a hospital bed. This days, my brother and me read that magazine every month.

Nouns, Determiners, and Pronouns: Forms and Usage

NOUNS

Nouns are words that refer to people, places, and things. Most nouns have both singular and plural forms.

SPELLING OF PLURAL FORMS

	SINGULAR	PLURAL
Most plural nouns simply end in *–s*.	student	students
Add *–es* to nouns ending in *–s*, *–ch*, *–sh*, *–x*, or *–z*.	match tax	match**es** tax**es**
When nouns end in *–f* or *–fe*, change the *–f* or *–fe* to *–v* and add *–es*. **Exception:** *beliefs*	shelf knife wife	shel**ves** kni**ves** wi**ves**
When nouns end in a consonant + *–y*, change the *–y* to *–ies*.	berry spy	ber**ries** sp**ies**
When nouns end in a vowel + *–y*, just add *–s*.	day	day**s**
When nouns end in *–o*, they may require an *–s* or an *–es* ending. Consult your dictionary if you're not sure which ending to use.	photo logo hero	photo**s** logo**s** hero**es**
Some nouns have **irregular plural forms**.	man child	**men** **children**
Some nouns are borrowed from **foreign languages**, so they keep the plural form of the original language.	analysis bacterium paparazzo phenomenon	analys**es** bacter**ia** paparazz**i** phenomen**a**

NOUNS THAT HAVE PLURAL FORMS ONLY

Some nouns appear in the plural form only. The objects or ideas might have two or more parts but are considered singular entities. Use plural verbs with these nouns.

binoculars　credentials　goods　scissors
clothes　(eye)glasses　savings　shorts

My **pants** are in the wash. My **glasses** are on the table.

PLURAL NOUNS WITH SINGULAR MEANINGS

Some nouns always have plural forms but singular meanings. Use third-person-singular verbs with these nouns.

economics　mathematics　mechanics
news　politics　physics

Physics is a difficult subject. The **news** appears online.

COUNT AND NONCOUNT NOUNS

Count nouns refer to people, places, and things that you can count, such as *girl* or *toy*. Count nouns have both singular and plural forms. **Noncount nouns** cannot be counted and have only singular forms.

Count: I own a **cellphone**. My brother has two **cellphones**.
Noncount: We have too much **homework**. **Money** changes people.

To express the quantity of a noncount noun, we use expressions that describe amounts, such as *types of*, *a lot of*, or *pieces of*. Note that the noncount noun remains singular.

pieces of information
I have two ~~informations~~.

Common Noncount Nouns

CATEGORIES OF OBJECTS		FOOD	NATURE AND SUBSTANCES	ABSTRACT NOUNS	
baggage	machinery	bread	air	advice	knowledge
clothing	mail	cheese	chalk	attention	luck
equipment	makeup	fish	coal	behaviour	patience
furniture	money	honey	electricity	education	publicity
homework	music	meat	fur	effort	proof
housework	postage	milk	hair	evidence	research
ink	software	rice	paint	health	time**
jewellery	wildlife	salt	radiation	help	trouble
luggage	work*	sugar	weather	information	violence

* *Work* is a noncount noun except when it refers to artistic works.
** *Time* is a noncount noun when it refers to free time or spare time.

DETERMINERS

DETERMINERS WITH COUNT AND NONCOUNT NOUNS

COUNT NOUNS (*many, few, a few*)	NONCOUNT NOUNS (*much, little, a little*)	COUNT AND NONCOUNT NOUNS (*a lot of*)
She has **very few*** friends. She has **a few**** friends. He has **many** friends.	She has **very little*** money. She has **a little**** money. He doesn't have **much***** money.	He has **a lot of***** friends and **a lot of** money.

* *Few* and *little* mean "almost none" and often indicate complaints.
** *A few* and *a little* mean "a small amount." There is no negative connotation.
*** Use *much* only in negative and question forms. In affirmative forms, use *a lot of* instead.

USING *THIS*, *THAT*, *THESE*, AND *THOSE*

TERM	USAGE	EXAMPLE
this (singular) **these** (plural)	Refers to things that are near the speaker in time or place.	**This** is a great summer. **These** days, it is sunny. **These** sunglasses that I'm wearing will protect me from UV rays.
that (singular) **those** (plural)	Refers to things that are far from the speaker in time or place.	Do you see **those** people in **that** store? In 2011, there were severe floods, so **that** was a difficult year.

PRONOUNS

Pronouns replace nouns, other pronouns, and noun phrases. A complete list of pronouns appears in *Avenues 3: Grammar Review Guide.*

SUBJECT PRONOUNS AND OBJECT PRONOUNS

A **subject pronoun** does the action and is usually followed by a verb. An **object pronoun** is affected by the action and is usually found after a verb or preposition. A sentence may have more than one subject or object.

subject pronoun — **She**; object pronoun — **them**; object pronoun — **it**

The professor talked to the students about her latest experiment.

(The professor = subject; students = object; her latest experiment = object)

POSSESSIVE ADJECTIVES AND POSSESSIVE PRONOUNS

Possessive adjectives describe nouns and appear before the nouns that they describe. **Possessive pronouns** replace possessive adjectives and nouns.

possessive adjective	possessive pronoun
Lola and Rick lost **their** passports.	Did you lose **yours**?

REFLEXIVE PRONOUNS

Use reflexive pronouns when the subjects doing the actions and the objects affected by the actions are the same people or things.

The small child dressed **herself**.
We helped **ourselves** to some coffee.

Practice

NOUNS: SPECIAL RULES

Each* and *Every

Use a singular noun after *each* and *every*.

Each **day**, Max cleans every **room** in his house.

One of the* and *Each of the

Use a plural noun after *one of the* and *each of the*.

That is one of the best **movies** I have ever seen! I love each of the **actors**.

Kind of*, *Sort of*, and *Type of

Always use the plural form of *kind of*, *sort of*, and *type of* when they refer to more than one kind, sort, or type. Also write the plural form of the noun that follows *of* unless it is a noncount noun.

There are many **kinds** of people in the world.
The store has several **types** of luggage. (*Luggage* is a noncount noun.)

TIP

Always Use Singular Forms of Adjectives

Adjectives have no plural form, so never add –s to adjectives.

simple, plausible
There must be some ~~simples, plausibles~~ explanations.

Sometimes nouns act as adjectives.

I have eight **dollars**.	She has a fifty-**dollar** shirt.
Dollar is a noun, and ends in –s.	*Dollar* acts as an adjective, and does not end in –s.

EXERCISE 1 PLURALS

Using the spaces provided, change words to the plural form, if necessary. If no plural form is needed, write *X* instead. If the word ends in *–y*, you may have to first change the *–y* to *–i*.

EXAMPLE: There are many different recording compan~~y~~ ies in Canada.

1. Every day_____, companies produce many type_____ of new_____ product_____. One of the most important role_____ of advertisers is to create brand_____ identity_____ that their customer_____ will love. An interesting example_____ involves the Canadian company Research In Motion (RIM). In 1999, Mike Lazaridis and Jim Balsillie formed the company. They were former mathematic_____ and physic_____ student_____.

2. RIM's first product was the BlackBerry. Wireless mobile_____ device_____ could send a lot of information_____ efficiently. The company soon made million_____ of dollar_____ selling the BlackBerry. Today, the company is worth about five billion_____.* During the early 2000_____, it was one of the fastest-growing company_____ in the world.

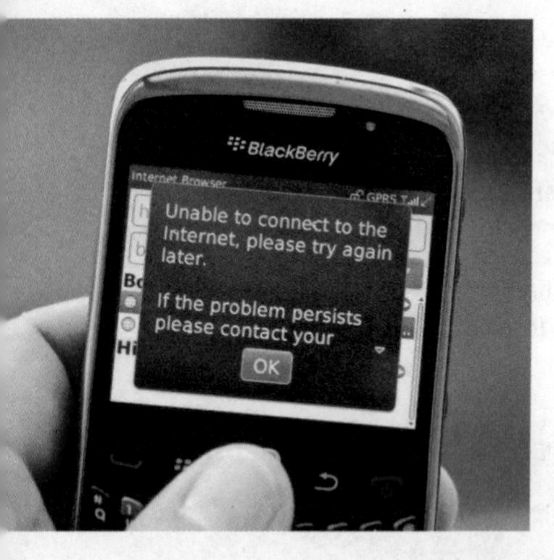

3. Since 2005, RIM has had a lot of severe_____ problems. One of the major issue_____ is a lack of vision. CEO Mike Lazaridis didn't listen to the advice_____ he was getting from many employee_____. In 2006, Steve Jobs created several_____ successful promotional_____ campaign_____ for the iPhone. The iPhone had many kind_____ of feature_____ such as a camera_____ and a lot of data_____ storage. Lazaridis lost touch with what each consumer_____ wanted from a cellphone. He thought people wanted the best-performing phone; he didn't realize he really needed to promote an image_____.

COLLECTIVE NOUNS

Collective nouns such as *army*, *family*, and *association* refer to groups that act as units. Therefore, any pronoun that refers to a collective noun is singular. (A list of collective nouns appears on pages 2–3.)

The government will not revise ~~their~~ **its** policies.

* With monetary values, sometimes the word *dollars* is implied but not written. Thus, the word before *dollars* remains singular.

TIP

Media: Singular or Plural?

Technically, the word *media* is the plural form of *medium*. However, many newspapers, magazines, and websites treat media as a collective singular noun. Some experts believe that the singular usage will soon become the standard.

If you talk about social media as a **type of mass communication**, use the singular form.

Social **media** has influenced the way people exchange information.

If you want to treat social media as **various communication tools**, then use the plural verb form.

Social **media**—Facebook, LinkedIn, and Twitter—have changed our world.

Note: Never write "medias."

EXERCISE 2 **SINGULAR OR PLURAL NOUNS**

Underline and correct fifteen errors involving plural forms in the following sentences.

EXAMPLE: The stores were filled with phones that were also musics (music) devices.

1. Most of us are obsessed with materials items. We constantly read about new type of gadget in the medias. For example, we can read news storeys on different e-readers. People used to get their informations from magazines or newspapers, but today, many can read the news on their smart phones. High-tech gadgets are a billion-dollars industry.

2. These days, many peoples think that a two-years-old cellphone is useless. Most phones can now take better photoes than digital cameras can. Consumers seem to need more stimuluses than ever before, which is why Apple's portable iPad has enjoyed such enormous success.

3. The heros of the younger generation are people such as Mark Zuckerberg and Bill Gates, the founders of tech giants Facebook and Microsoft. In fact, the paparazzis follow those men. When people read about the lifes of entrepreneurs such as Gates, they dream about owning million-dollars homes, too.

EXERCISE 3 DETERMINERS

PART A

Fill in the blanks with *much* or *many*.

1. These days, people provide too _______________ information to others. There have been _______________ instances in which someone has been embarrassed by a cellphone video. For example, there are _______________ stories on the Internet about the infamous "Dog Poop Girl" from Korea. She received too _______________ publicity for a silly mistake. While riding on a Seoul subway, she irritated _______________ fellow passengers because she refused to pick up her dog's poop. Another passenger didn't waste _______________ time before he put photos of her online. She received so _______________ negative attention that she dropped out of university.

PART B

Fill in the blanks with *little* or *few*.

2. The Internet has provided a new way for people to anonymously enforce social norms. In the past, there were only a _______________ ways to get shamed publicly for violating a social norm. Very _______________ people used to carry cameras, and there were very _______________ public security cameras. In the past, other passengers in the Dog Poop Girl's subway car might have gotten a _______________ uncomfortable, but they couldn't have shamed her in front of the whole world. Before smart phones and the Internet, there was very _______________ information available about people such as the Dog Poop Girl. A _______________ local newspapers and magazines might have carried the story, but people elsewhere would have paid very _______________ attention to the incident.

EXERCISE 4 *THIS, THAT, THESE, OR THOSE*

PART A

Underline and correct five errors involving *this*, *that*, *these*, or *those*. To review the rules for these determiners, see page 78.

EXAMPLE: These
<u>This</u> shoes that I'm wearing are too tight.

1. Do you see this shoe store across the street? Last year, something terrible happened to it. In September, football fans were angry when our local team

lost. At this time, I was in my apartment watching television. I heard people shouting, so I looked outside. I saw a mob of fans walking up our street. Some of these people were throwing stones. Then I heard a crashing sound. Rioters smashed the windows of the store and stole all of the shoes. The store owner felt angry about what had happened and said, "Why did that people destroy my window? This days, my insurance costs are too high, and I can't stay here anymore."

PART B

For each group of words in parentheses below, circle the best choice to complete the sentence.

EXAMPLE: I've been feeling quite lonely (these / those) days.

2. In the early 1800s, public shaming in Canada was common. Some (persons / people / peoples) were flogged in public for committing criminal acts. In (this / that / these / those) days, even branding was permitted as a form of punishment! At (this / that / these / those) time, the goal of the justice system was to punish rather than rehabilitate criminals. Now, (this / that / these / those) days, such brutal forms of punishment no longer exist in Canada.

PRONOUN AGREEMENT

A pronoun must agree with its **antecedent**, which is the word that the pronoun refers to.

antecedent pronoun

The Milgram experiment had **its** debut in 1961.

Subject Pronoun or Object Pronoun?

When a pronoun is paired with another noun, the correct choice of pronoun isn't always obvious. A simple way to determine the correct pronoun is to say the sentence with just that pronoun.

The professor asked Martin and (**I** or **me**) to present our topic.

Possible choices: The professor asked **I**. / The professor asked **me**.

Correct answer: The professor asked Martin and **me** to present our topic.

Pronouns in Comparisons

When a pronoun follows a comparison that uses *than* or *as*, ensure that you use the correct pronoun. To verify that your pronoun is correct, complete the thought.

I like psychology better than (**he** or **him**).

Complete the thought: I like psychology better than **he** (likes psychology).

TIP

Commonly Confused Words

The following pairs sound alike but have different meanings.

Its is a possessive adjective. ***It's*** is the contraction of "it is."

The store has **its** annual sale. **It's** a great time to shop.

Your is a possessive adjective. ***You're*** is the contraction of "you are."

You're late, but **your** excuse is original.

Their is a possessive adjective. ***There*** indicates that something exists.

There are many people who dislike **their** jobs.

Hal Niedzviecki

EXERCISE 5 MIXED PRONOUNS

Underline the appropriate words in parentheses.

EXAMPLE: My friend and (I / me) watched the video.

1. Hal Niedzviecki decided to embark on an interesting experiment. He allowed cameras to film (him / himself) twenty-four hours a day for the documentary *Peep Culture*. Filmmakers Sally Blake and Jeannette Loakman installed (theirselves / themselves / themself) in a studio near Niedzviecki's home, and they edited the footage that they received. The documentary was (there / their / theirs) idea, even though Niedzviecki was the subject. (He / Him) and his wife agreed to the project.
2. (There / Their / They) were many reasons Niedzviecki chose to make the documentary. (Her / His) book *The Peep Diaries* had made (her / him / himself) a minor celebrity after (she / it / he) was selected by Oprah Winfrey's magazine *O* as a must-read book in 2009. Before agreeing to do the documentary, Niedzviecki did not have a Facebook account, Twitter account, or blog. After agreeing to the documentary, (he / him) decided to get all three.
3. At first, Niedzviecki felt shy in front of the camera. Neither (he / him) nor his wife loved to be filmed constantly. It seemed like the producers were more excited about the project than (he / him) and his wife. Eventually, Hal became comfortable, and he started to consider what his viewers thought about (he / him). His wife said, "Hal was in front of the camera more than (I / me). I didn't let the filmmakers come upstairs."
4. Niedzviecki thinks that the downside of "peep" culture is that everybody wants to be famous. (Its / It's) detrimental to our social development. Think of all the aspects of (your / you're) life that are affected by peep culture.

PRONOUNS: SPECIAL RULES

Pronouns after *And, Or,* and *Nor*

When two or more nouns are joined by *and,* use a plural pronoun to refer to them.

Milgram **and** Zimbardo published **their** results.

When the nouns are joined by *or* or *nor*, the pronoun form is the same as the form of the noun that is nearest to it.

singular form
Does either Milgram **or** Zimbardo have regrets about **his** experiment?

plural form
Neither the man **nor** the women removed **their** glasses.

Pronouns after *One of the / Each of the*

In a sentence containing the expression *one of the* or *each of the*, the subject is the indefinite pronoun *one* or *each*. You must use a singular pronoun to refer to the subject.

One of the women spoke with **her** lawyer.

Indefinite Pronouns

When the antecedent is a singular indefinite pronoun such as *everybody*, *something*, or *nobody*, use a singular pronoun to refer to it.

At the men's club, nobody had a chance to voice **his** objection to the new rule.

If the gender of the subject is unknown, or if the subjects include both genders, use both the male and female pronouns. If the sentence then appears awkward, simply change the subject to the plural form.

Incorrect: Everybody must submit **their** answers to the professor.
Solution: Everybody must submit **his or her** answers to the professor.
Better solution: The students must submit **their** answers to the professor.

EXERCISE 6 WRITING PRONOUNS

Write the appropriate pronoun or possessive adjective in the blanks.

EXAMPLE: He conducted the experiment in his laboratory.

1. Solomon Asch was a social scientist. One of his most well-known experiments had __________ debut in 1951. In a small room, he conducted __________ classic study about conformity. He gathered a group, and __________ consisted of about ten participants. The people believed that __________ were in an experiment to test __________ visual judgment. Each person was led into a room filled with other people. What the participants didn't realize was that everybody else in the room had __________ role to play. In fact, all the participants were actors except for the subject. Everyone was shown a line, and then __________ had to state which line from among a new set was similar to the first line. The correct answer, B, would be obvious to the average person if __________ looked carefully.

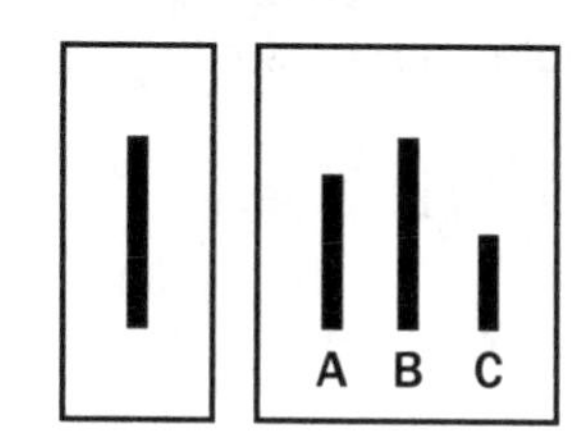

→

2. Everyone working for Asch knew that ____________ must give the wrong answer. Asch wanted to know if the unsuspecting subject would give the same incorrect answer as the others in the group. In the first test, a male subject listened to the other participants, and then made sure ____________ answer would match those of the others in the room. Neither the first nor the second male subject answered correctly, even though ____________ clearly knew what the correct answer was. In fact, over one-third of the subjects answered the question incorrectly because ____________ wanted to conform to the group. Those who disagreed with the others in the group expressed extreme discomfort. ____________ fidgeted, looked at ____________ hands, and appeared nervous.

AVOID VAGUE PRONOUNS

When you use pronouns, the antecedent (the person or object that the pronoun refers to) should be clear to the reader. Avoid using confusing pronouns such as *it* and *they* that have no clear antecedent.

Vague: They say that most people are conformists. (Who are *they*?)

Clearer: **Psychologists** say that most people are conformists.

Vague: It said in a magazine that some ads manipulate children. (Who or what is *it*?)

Clearer: **A magazine writer** claimed that some ads manipulate children.

In an essay that contains a repeated pronoun, such as *he* or *they*, make sure that the antecedents are clear.

Many teens try to be rebellious. Often, their actions worry their parents. They [**The parents**] surely want them to be happy and healthy. Sometimes discussions aren't enough for them [**the teens**]. They lose their [**their parents'**] trust and then they don't know what to do.

TIP

Consistent Point of View

When you write a paragraph or essay, make sure that your pronouns are consistent. Don't shift pronouns unless you're adding a supporting anecdote and the shift is logical.

Everyone needs to feel loved and respected. When people know that they are important to somebody else, it helps ~~you~~ [**them**] to make the correct decisions.

EXERCISE 7 **IDENTIFYING PRONOUN ERRORS**

Underline and correct twelve errors involving pronoun usage.

their
EXAMPLE: Our guests forgot to bring <u>there</u> smart phones.

1. In this high-tech age, some new psychological problems have come to light. If someone sends you a text message, do you respond to them immediately? Do you constantly write on you're Facebook wall? They say that compulsive texting may be a sign of a psychological addiction. It's also known that frequent Internet users experience cravings and withdrawal. If your online for several hours each day, you might have a problem.

2. Last summer, my partner Victor and me tried to avoid online social networks for one month. It was difficult for Victor and I. Our friends continued to post on there Facebook pages, but we resisted. My cousins Angela and Kaylee also tried to stop using social media. However, they were less successful than Victor and me. They both posted comments on there Facebook walls. In the end, we enjoyed the experience and concluded that people feel better when you're not tied to a schedule of checking Facebook and Twitter every few hours. Giving up some online activities was a great experience for Victor and I. We lived real lives instead of online lives. Facebook has it's benefits, but real life is even better.

UNIT Review

Complete the following exercises. If you don't know an answer, go back and review the appropriate section.

1. Underline the six noncount nouns in the list below. Remember that a noncount noun doesn't have a plural form.

advice	animal	assignment	children	dollar	equipment
homework	information	music	person	research	suitcase

2. Underline and correct the errors in the following sentences. Then write a rule about each error.

   a) He made a two-millions-dollar investment. ________________

   Rule:  ____ →

b) In 2009, I had a good year because this year, I earned a lot of money. ______________

Rule: ______________________________

c) I needed more informations about the product. ______________

Rule: ______________________________

d) There were less customers at the bank today than there were yesterday. ______________

Rule: ______________________________

3. For each sentence, underline the correct pronoun in parentheses.

a) You should lock (you're / your) car doors unless (it's / its) a very old vehicle.

b) Neither Jake nor his brother ate (his / their) supper.

c) Please don't try to sell that product to Tim and (I / me).

d) Everyone puts useless items in at least one of (their / his or her) kitchen drawers.

e) You earn more money than Bruno or (I / me).

My eLab

Need more practice? Visit My eLab and try additional grammar exercises.

Final Review

PART A

Underline the appropriate words in parentheses.

1. In the 1980s, people had a lot of privacy. In (this / these / those) years, nobody carried cellphones. If someone committed an illegal action, (they / he or she) could get away with it. But now, everything has changed. These days, many people's transgressions end up on YouTube. A new trend known as "Internet vigilantism" is sweeping cyberspace. (Much / Many) ordinary citizens have been affected by it.

2. For example, I was with some friends at a Stanley Cup hockey game. After the game, someone asked my friend and (I / me) to go to a club. On our way there, we entered a riot zone where people were breaking windows and robbing stores. We saw an acquaintance steal a few (piece / pieces) of (electronic / electronics) (equipment / equipments). Another friend was carrying two-(hundred /hundreds)-

(dollar / dollars) jeans. I was surprised by the stealing, but my friend was more shocked than (I / me). We wanted to leave the riot zone right away, but neither the bus nor the subway had (their / there / its / it's) schedule posted where we could easily see it. Finally, someone offered my friend and (I / me) a lift.

3. Later, we were very glad that we hadn't engaged in the looting. A Facebook group targeted rioters, and (their / its / it's) purpose was to name and shame them. In the past, police would have had very (few / little) (information / informations) about the rioters. But a few hours after the hockey riot, almost everybody had (their / his or her / they're) picture on Facebook. (Thousand / Thousands) of (persons / people / peoples) called the police with the names of rioters. One rioter was so depressed after her name appeared in the news, she underwent a three-(week / weeks) stay in a hospital. Police have some (advice / advices) for people who want to riot: think twice before acting.

PART B

Underline and correct five errors involving nouns, pronouns, or determiners.

4. Over the years, many riots have been described in the medias. In Andrew Potter's text, "Rioting Is Fun," he argues that everyone would riot if they could. According to Potter, most persons would enjoy stealing and looting. During a hockey riot, for instance, spectators might have very few control over their own responses. I disagree with Potter. If someone asked my friends and I to participate in a riot, we would refuse.

Material Possessions

Think about the most significant items that you own. Consider large items such as a car or smaller items such as a piece of jewellery, a photo, or an electronic item. In a team with two other people, share information about your belongings. Explain why you value certain items. Then, on a piece of paper, write a paragraph about your two partners and their items. List the material objects each person values, and describe their reasons for valuing those objects.

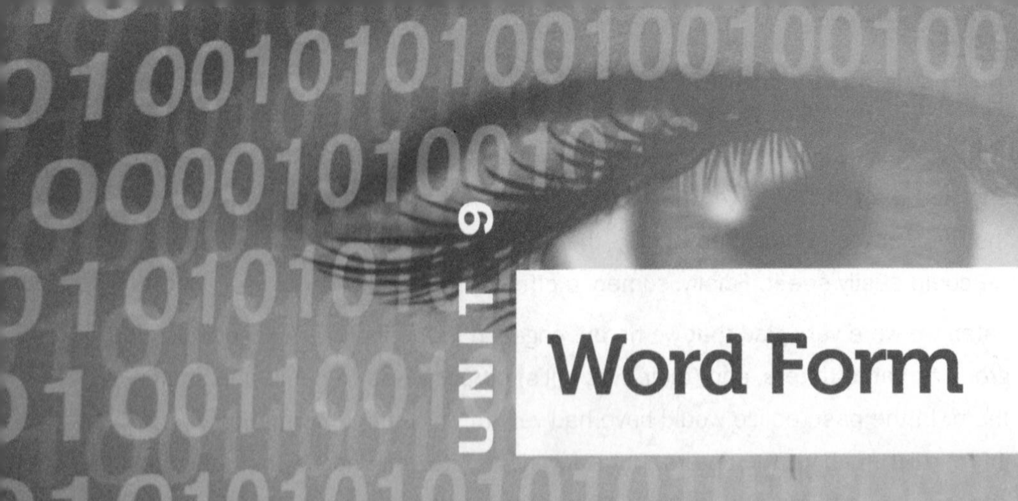

UNIT 9

Word Form

Preview

PASSIVE VOICE CHALLENGE

Verbs can be either **active** or **passive**. When a verb is passive, the subject does not perform an action. Instead, the subject is affected by the action.

Active: Chandra **made** the coffee.
Passive: The coffee **was made** by Chandra.

With a partner, rewrite the following sentences so that they are in the passive voice, but keep verb tenses consistent. Note that the "by *subject*" phrase is not always needed.

EXAMPLE: Active: Workers plant corn in the spring.
Passive: Corn is planted in the spring (by workers).

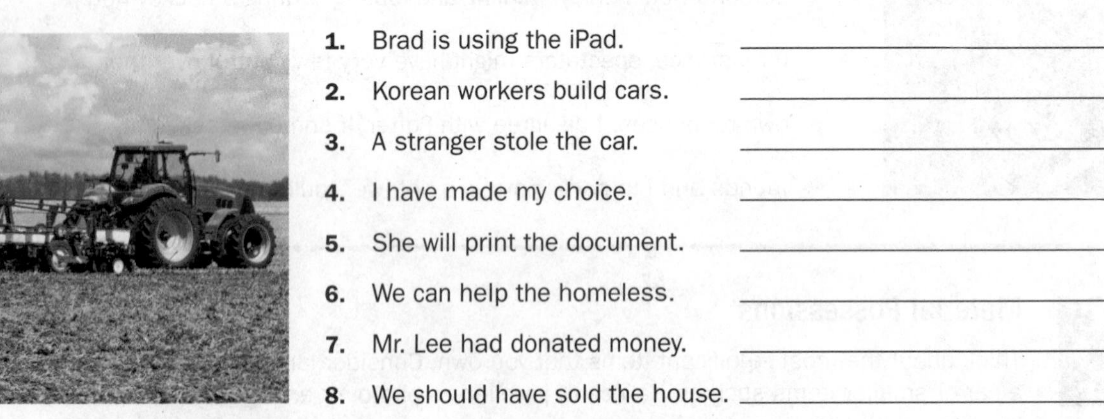

1. Brad is using the iPad. ______________________________
2. Korean workers build cars. ______________________________
3. A stranger stole the car. ______________________________
4. I have made my choice. ______________________________
5. She will print the document. ______________________________
6. We can help the homeless. ______________________________
7. Mr. Lee had donated money. ______________________________
8. We should have sold the house. ______________________________

Passive Voice: Forms and Usage

For the **passive voice**, use the verb *be* + the past participle. It is preferable to use the **active voice**—except when emphasizing an action, versus the doer of the action. Use the passive voice sparingly.

Kurt **wrote** that story in 1961.
This is active because the subject (Kurt) performed the action.

That story **was written** in 1961.
This is passive because the subject (the story) was affected by the action; the subject didn't perform the action.

ACTIVE AND PASSIVE FORMS

VERB TENSE OR MODAL	ACTIVE (The subject is acting.)	PASSIVE (The subject is affected by the action.) *be* + past participle
simple present	Max teaches spies.	Spies **are taught** by Max.
present progressive	is teaching	**are being taught**
simple past	taught	**were taught**
present perfect	has taught	**have been taught**
past perfect	had taught	**had been taught**
future	will teach	**will be taught**
can	can teach	**can be taught**
could	could teach	**could be taught**
should	should teach	**should be taught**
would	would teach	**would be taught**
must	must teach	**must be taught**
should (past form)	should have taught	**should have been taught**

To Be

Use the past participle after *to be*.

Children need **to be loved**.

Gerunds and Infinitives: Forms and Usage

GERUNDS AS SUBJECTS

Usually, the subject of a sentence is a noun. A gerund is an "ing" verb that functions as a noun.

Exercising is important for the health.

GERUNDS AND INFINITIVES

When a verb appears after another verb, use the infinitive form for the second verb most of the time. The infinitive consists of *to* + the base form of the verb. But note that some verbs should be followed by gerunds.

Infinitive: We **need to leave**.
Gerund: Ryan **enjoys singing**.

Some Common Verbs Followed by Gerunds

acknowledge, admit, adore, appreciate, avoid, can't help, can't stand

consider, delay, deny, detest, discuss, dislike, enjoy

finish, involve, justify, keep, loathe, mention, mind

miss, postpone, practise, quit, recall, recollect, recommend

regret, resent, resist, risk

Some Common Verbs Followed by Infinitives

afford	consent	hope	plan	swear
agree	decide	learn	prepare	threaten
appear	demand	manage	pretend	volunteer
arrange	deserve	mean	promise	want
ask	expect	need	refuse	wish
claim	fail	offer	seem	would like
compete	hesitate			

Some Common Verbs Followed by Gerunds or Infinitives

Some common verbs can be followed by either gerunds or infinitives. Both forms have the same meaning.

begin continue like love start

Gerund: He **continued lying.** **Infinitive:** He **continued to lie.**

Practice

EXERCISE 1 **IDENTIFYING ACTIVE OR PASSIVE VERBS**

Underline the appropriate verb form. Then indicate whether each answer is a passive verb or an active verb by writing either *P* or *A* in the blank.

EXAMPLE: Many soldiers (have disciplined / have been disciplined) P for disobeying an order.

1. During times of war, armies (have sent / have been sent) ____ soldiers on very dangerous missions. A soldier (can disobey / can be disobeyed) ____ an order only if he or she (asked / is asked) ____ to commit an illegal act. Even if soldiers (send / are sent) ____ on missions they are unlikely to survive, they still have to obey. If an order (doesn't obey / isn't obeyed) ____, the offending soldier (may arrest / may be arrested) ____.

2. There are many instances in which the "I was obeying orders" defence (has used / has been used) ____. For instance, in 1968, during the Vietnam War, American soldier Lieutenant William Calley (killed / was killed) ____ more than one hundred civilians. Later, he claimed that he (had ordered / had been ordered) ____ to kill "the enemy" by his superior officer. Military courts (oblige / are obliged) ____ to press criminal charges against soldiers who carry out unlawful orders. Calley (sentenced / was sentenced) ____ to life in prison. However, his prison sentence (reduced / was reduced) ____ by President Richard Nixon in 1970.

EXERCISE 2 ACTIVE AND PASSIVE VERBS

PART A

Rewrite the following sentences so that they're in the passive voice: Change the verbs to the passive form. Don't alter verb tenses. Note that you don't always have to include the "by *subject*" phrase.

EXAMPLE: The supervisor *spies* on the workers.
The workers are spied on (by the supervisor).

1. Sometimes employers *place* spy cameras in the workplace.

   Sometimes spy cameras ______________________________.

2. Last year, Mr. Roy *installed* three surveillance cameras.

   Last year, three surveillance cameras ______________________________.

3. The video cameras *filmed* some sleeping workers.

   Some sleeping workers ______________________________.

4. As a result, the boss *has fired* three technicians.

   As a result, three technicians ______________________________.

PART B

Rewrite the following sentences so that they're in the active voice. Change the verbs to the active form. Don't alter verb tenses.

EXAMPLE: The workers *are spied* on by the bosses.
The bosses spy on the workers.

5. For months, Ben's privacy *has been violated* by the cameras.

   For months, the cameras ______________________________.

6. Last week, a complaint *was made* to the police by Ben.

   Last week, Ben ______________________________.

7. The case *will be investigated* by the union.

   The union ______________________________.

8. Complaints about privacy *are often ignored* by companies.

   Companies often ______________________________.

THE BASE FORM VERSUS THE PAST PARTICIPLE

Use the past participle (e.g., *moved*, *broken*, *seen*)

- of passive verbs and verbs that follow *to be*;

  The study was **completed** in 2012. It needs to be **published**.

- of verbs that follow *have*, *has*, or *had* in the perfect tenses.

  I have **read** many reports. The professor has **written** many books.

→

Use the base form (e.g., *go, eat, talk*)

- of verbs that follow the single word *to* in infinitive forms;

  She wanted to **move** to a suburb.

- of verbs that follow *do, does,* or *did* in question and negative forms.

  Did the participants **complete** the questionnaire?

TIP

Verb Form

Sometimes *be* is suggested but not written.

Sometimes the passive form can be written with just the final verb. Look at the following sentence. It has the passive form, so the past participle must be used.

The cost of wheat, **grown** in Albert, has risen.

missing words: *which* ***is***

Never write *to don't*.

When you use a negative infinitive, just put *not* before the infinitive.

The hacker decided ~~to don't~~ **not to** steal credit card information.

EXERCISE 3 **IDENTIFYING WORD-FORM ERRORS**

Underline and correct ten word-form errors.

EXAMPLE: Milgram's experiment is include (included) in most psychology textbooks.

1. In 1961, Stanley Milgram wanted to understood why ordinary Germans massacred innocent Jewish civilians during World War II. He created an interesting experiment. In 1974, his article, "The Perils of Obedience," was publish. Since then, information about Milgram's study has appear in most psychology textbooks.

2. Milgram's experiment showed how far people would go to obeyed authority figures. Each participant in the experiment was ask to administer electric shocks to another person. The subjects didn't realized that the other person was an actor. A few participants decided to don't give more shocks as soon as they heard the other

person scream. However, most of them administered the highest voltages even when the other person screamed in pain.

3. Milgram's experiment, study by students around the world, demonstrates that people will harm others if they are under orders to do so. The experiment showed how people are influence by those in positions of authority. Many good people sometimes choose to don't listen to their own conscience.

TIP

Considered

Never write "considerated." It is not a word!

Milgram's study **considered** is ~~considerated~~ a classic.

CHOOSING *–ING* OR *–ED*

Some adjectives look like verbs because they end in *–ing* or *–ed*.

- When an adjective ends in *–ing*, it describes a quality of a person or thing.
  The **interesting** speaker described his experiences in Afghanistan.
- When an adjective ends in *–ed*, it describes a person or animal's expression or feeling.
  The **interested** audience listened carefully.

EXERCISE 4 **WORDS ENDING IN *–ING* OR *–ED***

Underline the correct word in each set of parentheses.

1. In the past, the Central Intelligence Agency (CIA) was a (respecting / respected) institution, and its work was (considering / considerated / considered) important for the security of the United States. But in the early 1950s, the agency made a (surprising / surprised) decision. It hired McGill psychologist Dr. Ewen Cameron to do mind-control experiments on (unsuspecting / unsuspected) patients. Dr. Cameron was well-(compensating / compensated) for his work.
2. During the 1950s and 1960s, many patients arrived at Montreal's Allan Memorial Institute who had been (considering / considerated / considered) suicide. The (uninforming / uninformed) patients were (treating / treated) with the hallucinogenic drug LSD. Of course, they had (frightening / frightened) hallucinations. They were not (giving / given) accurate information about their treatment. Some deaths were (associating / associated) with the experiments.
3. Eventually, the nature of the experiments was (exposing / exposed) by investigative journalists. The public was (disturbing / disturbed) by the news. Many of Dr. Cameron's colleagues were upset about his (disappointing / disappointed) conduct. Cameron tried to rebuild his (damaged / damaging) reputation. Eventually, CIA Director William Colby apologized for the agency's (shocking / shocked) actions.

GERUNDS AFTER VERBS

When a verb appears after another verb, use the **infinitive form** for the second verb most of the time. But remember that sometimes the second verb should be a **gerund**, or "ing" verb.

Infinitive: He **wants to leave**. He **hopes to graduate**.
Gerund: He **enjoys eating**. She **finished talking**.

EXERCISE 5 GERUNDS AND INFINITIVES

Underline the appropriate verb form in parentheses. Remember that some verbs can be followed by both gerunds and infinitives (in these cases, underline both choices). If necessary, review the information about gerunds and infinitives on pages 91–92.

1. A person may plan (to betray / betraying) his or her country for many reasons. According to Christopher Andrew, co-author of *The Sword and the Shield*, the acronym MICE explains why a person might agree (to become / becoming) a traitor. MICE stands for "money, ideology, compromise, and ego."

2. According to Andrew, some people enjoy (to spend / spending) money so much that they will betray their countries for cash. They can't resist (to have / having) extra luxuries. Others hope (to have / having) some excitement in their lives. They don't mind (to commit / committing) dangerous acts.
3. Sometimes people decide (to believe / believing) in another country's ideology. They promise (to support / supporting) a country with different political views. Others can't avoid (to be / being) manipulated. In a court case, a man identified only as "Max B." mentioned (to become / becoming) a spy because someone was blackmailing him.
4. When Andrew finished (to write / writing) his book, he was surprised by the response. People really like (to read / reading) about spies.

STOP, *REMEMBER*, AND *USED TO*

Some verbs—such as *stop*, *remember*, and *used to*—can be followed by either an infinitive or a gerund, but the meaning of the sentence changes depending on the verb form you use.

FORM	MEANING	EXAMPLE
stop + infinitive	To stop an action in order to do something else.	He **stops to buy** gas every Sunday.
stop + gerund	To stop doing something permanently.	I **stopped buying** cigarettes five years ago.

→

FORM	MEANING	EXAMPLE
remember + infinitive	To remember to perform a task.	Please **remember to lock** the door.
remember + gerund	To have a memory about a past event.	I **remember meeting** him in 2005.
used to + infinitive	To express a past habit or situation.	Eva **used to live** alone.
used to + gerund	To be accustomed to something.	Eva is **used to living** alone.

EXERCISE 6 **GERUNDS AND INFINITIVES**

Underline the appropriate verb form in parentheses.

1. When William was a teenager, he (used to play / used to playing) poker every day. He remembers (to feel / feeling) nervous the first time he played. Like many adolescents, he wanted (to look / looking) cool. After a few months, he enjoyed (to bet / betting) money on the games. He was soon (used to gamble / used to gambling). Almost daily, on his way home from school, he would stop (to gamble / gambling) at his friend's house.

2. About five years later, William subscribed to online casinos. He couldn't stop (to gamble / gambling). He was psychologically addicted, and he knew that he had (to do / doing) something. At one point, after he finished (to max out / maxing out) his credit card limits, he promised to quit (to play / playing) on casino sites. Still, whenever he was near the city's casinos, he would stop by a friend's house (borrowing / to borrow) some cash, and then he would gamble. His friend would say, "Please remember (to pay / paying) me back as soon as possible." William kept (betting / to bet) off and on for several more years.

3. On January 1, 2013, after his debts had reached critical levels, William realized that he needed (quitting / to quit). He decided (to take / taking) action right away. That night, he joined Gamblers Anonymous and stopped (to gamble / gambling). Nowadays, he (used to live / is used to living) without his habit. Sometimes he misses (to bet / betting), but then he remembers (to lose / losing) a lot of money and the respect of his friends and family. He hopes (to rebuild / rebuilding) his credit rating. He also plans (to grow / growing) up and behave like an adult. He wants to stop (to act / acting) immature.

PREPOSITIONS PLUS GERUNDS

Many sentences have the structure *verb + preposition + object*. Therefore, a gerund can be the object of a preposition.

She is tired of **working** nights.

Some Common Verbs + Prepositions Followed by Gerunds

accuse of	(be) enthusiastic about	insist on	(be) responsible for
be accustomed to	(be) excited about	(be) interested in	succeed in
apologize for	feel like	look forward to	think about
contribute to	(be) fond of	(be) nervous about	(be) tired of
discourage him from*	forgive me for*	prevent him from*	(be) worried about
dream of	(be) good at	prohibit from	

* Certain verbs are followed by a noun or pronoun plus a preposition.

EXERCISE 7 PREPOSITIONS AND GERUNDS

Fill in the blanks with the correct preposition + gerund of the verbs in parentheses.

EXAMPLE: Harry Harlow was enthusiastic (study) about studying the importance of love in a scientific context.

1. Before the 1960s, experts believed that mothers were excited (raise) ____________ children and that breastfeeding contributed (create) ____________ the maternal bond. They also thought that showing affection to children was sentimental and had no real role in child-rearing. Psychologist Harry Harlow was interested (test) ____________ those ideas. He was accustomed (look) ____________ at conventional ideas in original ways. Clearly, Harlow was very good (find) ____________ interesting subjects for his experiments.

2. First, Harlow insisted (use) ____________ baby rhesus monkeys and separating them from their mothers. He prevented the baby monkeys (interact) ____________ with the outside world. Then he provided them with two fake mothers. One "mother" was made of soft cloth but had no food, while the other was made of coarse wire but had an attached bottle of milk. Harlow expected the "bottle mother" to get more attention from the babies, but, in fact, they were more interested (hug) ____________ the "cloth mother." When the cloth mother was removed from their cages for long periods, the baby monkeys would freeze up, scream, or cry.

3. Harlow was accused (be) ____________ cruel to the monkeys. He claimed that he never looked forward (hurt) ____________ the baby

monkeys, but, at the same time, he never apologized (deprive) ________________ ________________ them of a real mother and for stressing them intentionally to study their reactions. Ultimately, Harlow's study was responsible (change) ________________ the perceptions of people in the scientific community. These days, everyone acknowledges the immense importance of a parent's caresses and affection. Eventually, Harlow became an alcoholic and was estranged from his own children. Nonetheless, his study succeeded (demonstrate) ________________ that babies and young children need affection to develop properly.

UNIT Review

Complete the following exercises. If you don't know an answer, go back and review the appropriate section.

1. For each of the following sentences, fill in the blank with the passive form of the verb *sell* in the appropriate tense.

EXAMPLE: Every day, many books <u>are sold</u>.

a) Last week, a new article ________________ by the journalist.

b) Next year, a new book ________________ by Simmons Press.

c) Since 1990, over five hundred books ________________ by Simmons Press.

2. For each verb in parentheses, write either the gerund or infinitive form, as appropriate, in the space provided.

Amber Redmond enjoys (fly) ________________. She wants (become) ________________ a pilot. She hopes (get) ________________ her pilot's licence next March. Her mother said, "Stop (take) ________________ those lessons." However, Amber will finish (study) ________________ next month. She will become a pilot, and her mother can't prevent her from (do) ________________ it.

3. Underline and correct the error in each sentence.

a) Last year, Raoul developed a severe cough, so he stopped to smoke. Now he is a non-smoker.

b) Sophie tries to don't eat a lot of meat.

c) Raoul hates exercise, and he refuses walking in the woods.

d) Sophie avoids to be in the house while Raoul practises playing folk songs.

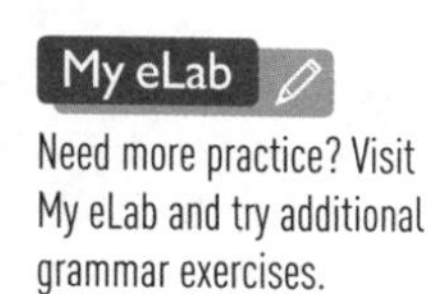

Need more practice? Visit My eLab and try additional grammar exercises.

Final Review

PART A

Underline the appropriate words in parentheses.

EXAMPLE: I would like (to know / knowing) more about the Omar Khadr case.

1. Do you remember (to hear / to hearing / hearing) about the Omar Khadr case? Although I usually avoid (to read / reading) about war, I am interested (to learning / learning / in learning) more about his situation. It is a complex case that has attracted a lot of controversy. Khadr was accused (to kill / killing / of killing) an American soldier in Afghanistan when he was only fifteen years old. In 2010, he was convicted of five charges.

2. Before Khadr's trial, many organizations, including UNICEF and the Canadian Bar Association, asked Canada (intercede / to intercede / to interceding) on Khadr's behalf because he was (considering / considerated / considered) a child at the time of his crimes. The Canadian government decided (to leave / leaving / for leaving) him in the United States. Some (informing / informed) members of the public were (surprising / surprised) by the Canadian government's (disturbed / disturbing) decision. Khadr's supporters did not succeed (to convincing / convincing / in convincing) government officials to change their minds. A 2004 documentary did not help Khadr's case. In the documentary, his mother and sister complained about Canada's liberalism and acknowledged (to feel / feeling / in feeling) pleased about the 9/11 attacks on the World Trade Center. At that point, some members of the public stopped (to care / caring) about Khadr.
3. What is your opinion about child war combatants? Some people argue that a fifteen-year-old boy can't help (to do / doing) what his father asks him to do. It's likely that no child enjoys (to live / living) in a war zone. Can a fifteen-year-old refuse (to follow / following) his parents' wishes? In Khadr's case, could he have stopped (to fight / fighting) and then left Afghanistan? Perhaps he was (used to live / used to living) amid violence and did not know what a normal childhood is. In the future, I hope (living / to live) in a less violent world. Perhaps, one day, people will believe that the murder of innocents can never be (justify / justified).

PART B

Make the following sentences passive. Don't alter verb tenses.

EXAMPLE: American soldiers arrested Khadr.
Khadr was arrested (by American soldiers).

4. In 2008, Michelle Shephard published a book about Khadr.
In 2008, a book about Khadr ______________________________
______________________________.

5. Many stores sell the book.
The book ______________________________
______________________________.

6. US interrogators may have tortured more prisoners.
More prisoners ______________________________
______________________________.

7. Eventually, authorities will release Khadr.
Eventually, Khadr ______________________________
______________________________.

8. Khadr's case has influenced international law.
International law ______________________________
______________________________.

Edit a Letter

In the letter below, the writer overuses the passive voice. The letter would be clearer if the writer had used the active voice. With a partner, underline the passive verbs, and then rewrite the letter using the active voice.

Your e-mail has been received by us. You will be contacted by a support technician soon. Your problem will be solved by our technician. Additionally, your account will be credited and you will be provided with two months of free support. If you have any further questions, we can be contacted during working hours.

____
____
____
____
____
____
____

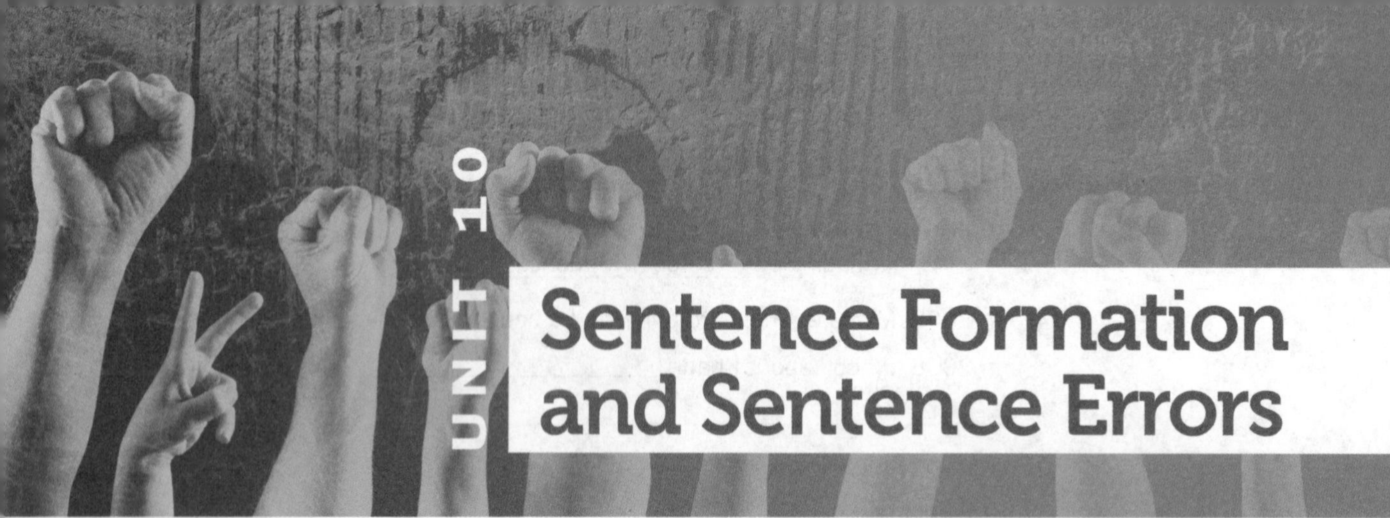

UNIT 10 Sentence Formation and Sentence Errors

Preview

IDENTIFY SENTENCE ERRORS

Write *C* next to sentences that are correct. Correct the errors in the other sentences.

1. Do you know what is the most important thing in life?
2. Friends and family are important, these connections help us navigate the world.
3. For example, dealing with a tragedy.
4. To get through a crisis, we must understand ourselves, accept our limits, and maintaining an optimistic attitude.
5. The final step is to accept what we can't change.
6. Because we must be realistic when we face the future.

Sentences: Forms and Usage

To make your writing more interesting, you can combine sentences in a variety of ways. Review the following sentence types.

SIMPLE SENTENCES

A simple sentence has one **independent clause** (complete idea).

The fraud victims went to court.

COMPOUND SENTENCES

A compound sentence contains two or more independent clauses—or complete ideas—joined by a coordinating conjunction such as *and*, *but*, *or*, *nor*, and *yet*. You can also combine complete ideas with a semicolon. A third way to create a compound sentence is to join complete ideas with a semicolon and transitional expression such as *furthermore*, *however*, and *therefore*.

independent clause / independent clause

Some rioters broke the law, **and** they were arrested.

Some rioters broke the law**;** they were arrested.

Some rioters broke the law**; therefore,** they were arrested.

COMPLEX SENTENCES

A complex sentence contains at least one independent clause and one **dependent clause**. A dependent clause begins with a subordinator or a relative pronoun.

A **subordinator** joins the secondary idea to the main idea. Following is a list of common subordinators.

after	because	even though	when
although	before	unless	whereas

dependent clause / independent clause

Because they worry about the environment, they held a protest.

independent clause / dependent clause

Some students will complain **when** tuition fees increase.

A **relative pronoun** describes a noun or pronoun. The most common relative pronouns include the following:

that which who whom whomever whose

independent clause / dependent clause

The rioter threw a rock **that** broke a window.

COMPOUND COMPLEX SENTENCES

To further add variety to your writing, you can also combine compound and complex sentences. The next example is a compound complex sentence.

complex sentence: Although Edward is shy, he is strong,

Although Edward is shy, he is strong, and he is a very effective police officer.

compound sentence: he is strong, and he is a very effective police officer.

COMMON SENTENCE ERRORS

FRAGMENTS

A fragment is an incomplete sentence. It is missing a subject, a verb, or a main clause. To correct a fragment, add the missing part or join it to another sentence. Review the following fragments and possible corrections.

	FRAGMENT	POSSIBLE CORRECTIONS
no subject	Have no children.	**Add a subject:** **Many couples** have no children.
no verb	First, the crime rate.	**Add a verb:** First, the crime rate **is dropping**.
no main clause	Because* he was hungry.	**Add a main clause:** **He stole food** because he was hungry.

* A subordinator such as *because* introduces a secondary idea. Make sure that your sentence also has a primary idea.

RUN-ON SENTENCES

A run-on sentence occurs when two complete ideas are joined incorrectly by a comma. Review the following run-on and some possible corrections.

RUN-ON SENTENCE	POSSIBLE CORRECTIONS
Jeremy left prison, he found a job.	**Add a coordinator:** Jeremy left prison, **and** he found a job.
	Add a subordinator: **After** Jeremy left prison, he found a job.
	Add a semicolon: Jeremy left prison; he found a job.
	Make two complete sentences: Jeremy left prison**. He** found a job.

Practice

SUBORDINATORS

Review some common subordinators.

SUBORDINATORS	PURPOSE	EXAMPLE
as **because** **so that**	Indicate a reason or cause	He learned karate **because** he wanted to be physically fit.
after **until** **before** **when**	Indicate a time	**After** he received his black belt, he returned to America.
as long as **if** **unless**	Indicate a condition	He will not fight with a stranger **unless** he feels threatened.
although **even though** **whereas**	Indicate a contrast	**Although** karate is difficult to learn, millions of people study it every year.

EXERCISE 1 COORDINATORS AND SUBORDINATORS

Underline the appropriate coordinating or subordinating conjunctions in parentheses.

EXAMPLE: Many quotes are attributed to famous people, (but / or / so) they are often wrong.

1. (When / Whereas / Although) Marie Antoinette moved to France, she had to adapt to a new culture. Many French citizens distrusted her (because / and / although) she was originally from Austria. Every morning, she would wear diamonds, (but / or / so) she would wear emeralds. She wanted to be good, (but / so / or) she sometimes visited poor neighbourhoods. At the same time, she lived in a palace (where / when / although) excessive luxury was the norm.

2. Marie Antoinette is one of the most famous queens in history, (or / so / but) she is not well known for a good reason. She is remembered for saying, "Let them eat cake." (Although / As long as / When) the phrase is popularly attributed to Marie Antoinette, some historians don't believe she said it. The phrase appeared in a book written (yet / when / so) she was only nine years old. The phrase also appeared in a book eight years before her birth, (so / but / or) she could not have been the first one to say it. These days, almost nobody knows King Louis XVI (unless / as long as / whereas) everyone has heard of Marie Antoinette.

RELATIVE CLAUSES

A relative clause is a dependent clause that is introduced by a relative pronoun. The following are some common relative pronouns and their purposes.

RELATIVE PRONOUNS	PURPOSE	EXAMPLE
that	Gives information about people or things	The project **that** I completed was easy.
which	Gives additional (non-essential) information about things	The movie, **which** has become a classic, stars Colin Farrell.
who **whom**	Give information about people (*Whom* is used in formal English to represent the object of a verb.)	The girl **who** lives next door is very nice. The man **who(m)** I met is married.
whose	Shows possession (*Whose* can replace *his*, *her*, *its*, or *their.*)	I met a man **whose** leg was broken.

TIP

Using *That* or *Which*

Both *that* and *which* refer to things, but *which* refers to non-essential ideas. In addition, *which* can imply that you are referring to the complete subject and not to just part of it. Compare the next two sentences.

The shirts **that** had stains provided DNA evidence.
(This sentence suggests that some shirts had no stains.)

The shirts, **which** had stains, provided DNA evidence.
(This sentence suggests that all of the shirts had stains.)

TIP

Commas with *Which*

Generally use commas to set off *which* clauses.

> The rescue, which cost a lot, was well organized.

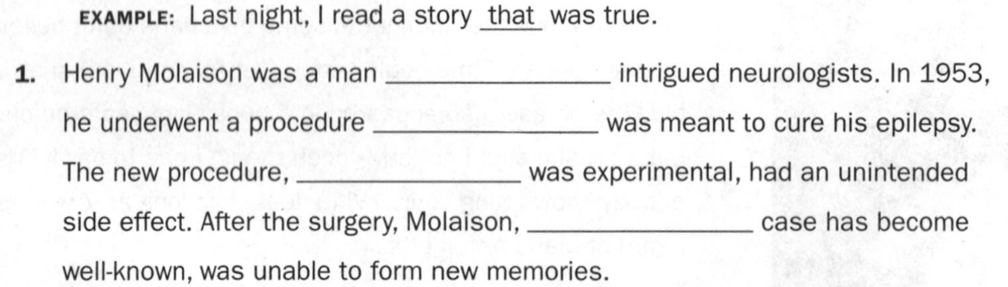

EXERCISE 2 **RELATIVE CLAUSES**

Fill in the blanks with *who*, *whom*, *that*, *which*, or *whose*. Note that in some cases, more than one answer is possible.

EXAMPLE: Last night, I read a story that was true.

1. Henry Molaison was a man ________________ intrigued neurologists. In 1953, he underwent a procedure ________________ was meant to cure his epilepsy. The new procedure, ________________ was experimental, had an unintended side effect. After the surgery, Molaison, ________________ case has become well-known, was unable to form new memories.

2. By studying Molaison, psychologists and researchers learned certain things ________________ they had never discovered before. One test, ________________ was performed in the mid-1950s, involved giving Molaison meals. A researcher ________________ Molaison didn't recognize put a plate of food on the table in front of him. Molaison ate. A few minutes later, the researcher put another plate on the table and said, "Mealtime." Molaison, ________________ had forgotten about his previous meal, happily ate another helping. Molaison, ________________ appetite was strong, felt full only after three meals.

3. A few years ago, I saw a movie ________________ was about an amnesiac. The movie, ________________ was excellent, was called *Memento*. The main character, ________________ name I don't remember, had a condition similar to Molaison's. *Memento*, ________________ has become a cult classic, is a fascinating film about memory.

COMMONLY CONFUSED WORDS

Who's and Whose

Who's is the contracted form of *who is*.	**Who's** at the door?
Whose indicates possession and replaces *his*, *her*, *its*, and *their*.	**Whose** car is that?

Who and Whom

Who is the subject of a clause.	The detective **who** specializes in arson wrote a book.
Whom is the object of a clause.	The detective **whom** we met was helpful.

Than, Then, and That

Than is used to compare two things.	She is older **than** I am.
Then means "at a particular time."	He graduated and **then** found a job.
That introduces a clause.	The book **that** I read is very good.

TIP

Which

Ensure that you spell *which* correctly.

which
The blog, ~~wich~~ is new, discusses patriotism.

EXERCISE 3 **IDENTIFYING ERRORS**

Underline and correct fifteen usage and spelling errors involving *who*, *whom*, *which*, *than*, *then*, *that*, *who's*, and *whose*.

who
EXAMPLE: There are many people which have contributed to revolutions.

1. Wael Ghonim is a man which played an important role in the Egyptian revolution of 2011. Ghonim supported slain protesters who's only crimes were opposing the regime of dictator Hosni Mubarak. Specifically, Ghonim's Facebook page, "We Are All Khaled Said," supported a young man whom was killed while in police custody. Ghonim, a young computer entrepreneur working for Google, became a symbol for the young protesters, most of who were educated and tech-savvy. His web page helped organize the protests than occurred nightly.

2. Ghonim's criticism of the Egyptian government, wich angered President Mubarak, resulted in Ghonim's arrest. After he was released from jail, he appeared on a television show who was seen by millions of Egyptians. During the interview, what was shown on the Dream TV 2 network in Egypt, Ghonim talked about his cyber-activism. He said than he was proud of the protesters in the streets. Than, the next day, the number of protests escalated.

3. It was the public's anger than eventually brought down the Mubarak government on February 11, 2011. Afterwards, everyone wondered, "Whose going to lead the nation?" These days, Ghonim, whose respected and admired, doesn't feel like a hero. According to him, the people who's lives were lost are the true heroes of the revolution. The transition to democracy, which is not quite complete, has been difficult. Ultimately, the Egyptian revolution, who was quite violent, has changed the political climate of the Middle East forever.

TRANSITIONAL EXPRESSIONS

Transitional expressions show the progression of ideas in an essay. You can place them at the beginning of sentences, and you can also use them to join two complete ideas.

Begin a sentence: However, the game was over.
Join complete ideas: Ray was losing the fight; however, he kept trying.

Some Common Transitional Expressions

Chronology:	first	second	finally	suddenly
Addition:	additionally	also	furthermore	moreover
Emphasis:	above all	clearly	of course	undoubtedly
Comparison:	however	in contrast	nevertheless	similarly
Conclusion:	in conclusion	in short	therefore	thus
Example:	for instance	in fact	for example	

Note: A more complete list of transitional words and expressions appears in Appendix 4, on page 178 of *Avenues 3: English Skills*.

TIP

Although or *However*

Do not confuse *although* and *however*. ***Although*** is a subordinator that means "even though." Don't put a comma after *although*. ***However*** is a transitional expression. Always put a comma after *however*.

Although he broke the law, he didn't go to jail.
He broke the law; **however,** he didn't go to jail.
He broke the law. **However,** he didn't go to jail.

EXERCISE 4 SUBORDINATORS AND TRANSITIONAL EXPRESSIONS

Fill in the blanks with a subordinator or transitional expression from the list below. Use each choice once. The first one has been done for you as an example.

~~although~~	however	on the other hand	undoubtedly
eventually	meanwhile	subsequently	until
furthermore	nevertheless	thus	whereas

1. Dan Ariely, a professor of psychology at Duke University, has written about honesty in his book *The (Honest) Truth about Dishonesty*. ___Although___ most people like to believe that they are honest, they frequently fool themselves. ________________, people from all classes and in all societies may be dishonest sometimes.
2. In April 2011, college student Dan Weiss was hired by the Kennedy Center for the Performing Arts in Washington, DC. His job was to take the stock inventory

at the centre's gift shop. ____________________, about three hundred well-intentioned volunteers worked at the shop. The shop sold $400,000 of merchandise. ____________________, about $150,000 was disappearing each year. The gift shop had no cash registers, just a cash box that volunteers put the money into.

3. Weiss was determined to find the thief. ____________________, the thief was one of the volunteers. He suspected a young man who brought the cash box to the bank each night. Weiss set up a sting operation, putting some marked bills into the box. Then, one night, Weiss and a detective waited patiently in a bush outside the bank ____________________ the shop closed. Later, when the young volunteer left the bank, they searched him. He had $60 of marked bills in his pocket. ____________________, he was fired from his job. ____________________, the thefts continued. ____________________, there had to be other thieves.

4. ____________________ Weiss discovered that hundreds of the volunteers were pilfering objects or money. He decided to put a cash register and an itemized logbook into the gift shop. Before, money disappeared every day ____________________ after the cash register was installed, no money disappeared. From this story, we can learn the following lesson. On the one hand, all types of people can be dishonest. ____________________, people's bad behaviour can easily be modified.

EXERCISE 5 CHOOSING THE RIGHT WORD

Underline the appropriate word in parentheses.

EXAMPLE: I read a story (who / that) was sad.

1. I read a story about a man (who's / whose) life was very difficult. Mohamed Bouazizi was a Tunisian street vendor (who / who's / whose) wares were continually taken by the police. He lived in a city (who / where / what) ordinary citizens were continually harassed. On the morning of December 16, 2010, he borrowed about US$200 to buy produce (who / where / that) he would sell at the market. As usual, a police officer, (whom / whose / who's) Bouazizi recognized, appeared on the street. (However / Although) street-cart vendors didn't need permits, the officer asked to see one. Bouazizi did not have money to bribe the officer; (therefore / because / although), the officer took Bouazizi's electronic weighing scale and tossed his produce on the ground.

→

2. That afternoon, the twenty-seven-year-old man, (whose / who / whom) heart was racing, ran to the governor's office to complain. He asked for his weighing scale back; (although / however), he was ignored. In desperation, Bouazizi bought a can of gasoline from a gas station (who / that) was nearby. Then he set himself on fire.
3. Bouazizi's self-immolation was the catalyst (who / when / that) sent protesters into the streets. For weeks, they gathered in squares. (However / Although) the Tunisian president, Ben Ali, visited Bouazizi in the hospital, it didn't help the president's reputation. One month later, in January, Ben Ali fled the country, (who / what / which) was a wise choice. Today, he is a man (who's / whose / which) living a life of luxury in Saudi Arabia. In the meantime, Tunisia is a nation (who / that / who's) is building a democracy.

CONSTRUCTING EMBEDDED QUESTIONS

It is possible to combine a question with a statement or to combine two questions. The result, an embedded question, is set within a larger sentence. Such embedded questions do not require the usual question word order, added auxiliaries, or, in some cases, even question marks. As you review the following examples, pay attention to word order.

Question	**Embedded Question**
Why do people commit crimes?	He asked why people commit crimes.
How should we proceed?	I wonder how we should proceed.

Use *if* or *whether* if there is no question word, or if the question word is not suitable in the embedded question.

Was he convicted?	Do you know **if** he was convicted?

TIP

Use the Correct Word Order

When you edit your writing, ensure that you have formed any embedded questions properly.

she thought

Dr. Alvarez wonders why ~~do~~ people commit crimes. I asked her what ~~did she think~~ about the issue.

EXERCISE 6 CREATING EMBEDDED QUESTIONS

Complete the following embedded questions.

EXAMPLE: What does he want? I wonder what he wants.

1. How old is the suspect? Do you know ______
2. Why was she arrested? I wonder ______
3. Does she have an alibi? Can you tell me ______
4. Where did the crime occur? I don't know ______
5. Should we watch the trial? I wonder ______
6. What will the jury decide? We discussed ______

The president of Russia Vladimir Putin and former Egyptian president Hosni Mubarak

EXERCISE 7 IDENTIFYING EMBEDDED-QUESTION ERRORS

Underline and correct six errors involving embedded questions.

EXAMPLE: The writer explains how ~~can people~~ people can hold on to power for so long.

1. Around the world, citizens wonder why are so many nations run by dictators and authoritarian regimes. They also question how were certain leaders able to accumulate their wealth. For example, people want to know how did former Egyptian president Hosni Mubarak become so wealthy.

2. To understand the former Egyptian president's wealth, people should consider why was Mubarak admired and supported by the international political community during his reign. Around the world, democratic Western nations tend to support undemocratic regimes when it is good for international business. For example, if someone wonders how could Mubarak have remained in power for eighteen years, he or she should evaluate the situation. About 4 percent of the world's oil supply must pass by boat through the Suez Canal in Egypt. Perhaps that explains why did Mubarak ensure business went smoothly for the companies and nations that needed to use the canal. He established mutually beneficial friendships with international leaders.

IDENTIFYING FRAGMENTS AND RUN-ON SENTENCES

A sentence must have a subject and a verb, and it must express a complete idea.

A **fragment** is an incomplete sentence.

A **run-on sentence** occurs when two or more complete sentences are incorrectly connected. Note that you can't join two complete sentences with a comma. Also note that very long sentences are not necessarily run-ons.

Fragment:	Although there was no evidence.
Run-on:	The case went to court**,** the eyewitness was compelling.
Complete sentence:	Although there was no evidence, the case went to court **because** the eyewitness was compelling.

TIP

Adding Examples

When you add an example to prove a point, be particularly careful that your new sentence is complete. The next fragments were taken from student essays.

For example, when they made the prisoners clean toilets in "The Stanford Prison Experiment."

Like Milgram's experiment when people obeyed an authoritarian figure.

EXERCISE 8 FRAGMENTS AND RUN-ONS

For the following sentences, write *F* beside the ones that are fragments and *RO* beside the run-ons. Write *C* beside the sentences that are correct.

EXAMPLE: The streets were quiet. C

Because soldiers patrolled them. F

1. Because street vendor Mohamed Bouazizi lit himself on fire. ____
2. He wanted to protest against the Tunisian government. ____
3. Which sparked a cultural revolution. ____
4. Riots erupted in the Middle East, cities burned. ____
5. Until the end of 2011. ____
6. Activists living under the repressive regime took a chance and decided to fight for change. ____
7. The Tunisian government fell, nobody knew who would lead the nation. ____
8. For example, when the president resigned and fled the country. ____
9. Social media played a role, students communicated using Facebook. ____

Manoubia Bouazizi, mother of Mohamed Bouazizi, posing with a poster of her late son

EXERCISE 9 IDENTIFYING SENTENCE ERRORS

Underline and correct ten sentence errors involving fragments and run-ons. Use a variety of correction methods. Note that there may be more than one way to correct the errors.

EXAMPLE: The case was over; the defendant was innocent.

1. There are many debates about acceptable behaviour during political protests. Such as the question of the legitimacy of violent action. Some activists believe in passive resistance, others feel that aggressive force is sometimes necessary.

2. In 2010, some protestors at the G20 Toronto Summit committed acts of vandalism and looting, police responded forcefully. The largest mass-arrest in Canadian history. Since then, many activists have criticized police tactics. Which included intimidation and even assault. However, others have supported the police, they want the vandals to be punished. Some of the G20 protestors received prison sentences. Including Alex Hundert. He was arrested before the protests even started and was charged with conspiracy.

3. During Quebec's 2012 student strikes, most of the protesters were peaceful, however, others were not. On May 10, 2012, smoke bombs were thrown into three subway stations. Causing chaos. Citizens were divided. Some supported the student protestors, others criticized protestors' actions.

FAULTY PARALLEL STRUCTURE

Pairs or groups of items in a sentence should have a balanced grammatical structure within that sentence. Faulty parallel structure occurs when equivalent ideas are presented with different grammatical structures.

Not parallel: The detectives worked slowly and were careful.
Parallel adverbs: The detectives worked slowly and carefully.

Not parallel: They were people who were trained, who were professional, and having high standards.
Parallel clauses: They were people who were trained, who were professional, and who had high standards.

To identify faulty parallel structures in a sentence, look at the repeated grammatical units and then rewrite the unit that isn't parallel to the others.

EXERCISE 10 **FAULTY PARALLEL STRUCTURE**

Underline and correct the parallel structure error in each sentence. Write *C* beside the sentences that are correct.

EXAMPLE: I enjoy reading and to learn about psychology. learning

1. Aggressive behaviour can involve bodily contact such as biting, hitting, or to push. ____________
2. In fact, aggression can be physical or verbal. ____________
3. In the 1930s, some doctors, psychologists, and people who do research tried to identify the causes of aggressive behaviour. ____________
4. The scientists thought that their work was exciting and a challenge. ____________
5. In 1939, experimenters removed the temporal lobe from some monkeys that were friendly, active, and who had good health. ____________
6. After the surgeries, the monkeys showed no fear of snakes or humans. ____________
7. The doctors determined that the amygdala plays a role that is essential and has significance in fear responses. ____________
8. The scientists hoped to learn more about how humans anticipate and dealing with fear. ____________
9. In 1966, a man named Charles Whitman acted strangely and with violence. ____________
10. Before his death in a shootout with police, Whitman wrote a note and was asking doctors to examine the state of his brain. ____________
11. In fact, a later examination revealed the presence of a tumour next to his amygdala. ____________
12. Scientists believe that damage to the frontal lobe can contribute to behaviour that is controlling, sadistic, and causes people to abuse others. ____________

UNIT Review

Correct the errors in the following sentences. Then write a rule explaining each error. If you don't know an answer, go back and review the appropriate section.

1. First, the strangest experiment.

   Rule: ______________________________

2. A scientist conducted a test who was very successful.

   Rule: ______________________________

3. The test was about altruistic behaviour, it was fascinating.

   Rule: ______________________________

4. I wondered why did they create the test.

   Rule: ______________________________

5. The researcher was helpful, friendly, and acted with generosity.

   Rule: ______________________________

My eLab

Need more practice? Visit My eLab and try additional grammar exercises.

Final Review

PART A

For each of the sentences, circle the letter of the answer that best fills in the blank. Note that *X* means "nothing."

1. Facebook and Twitter have a role in revolutions ___ activists use them to organize protests.

   a) , b) ; c) : d) X

2. Malcolm Gladwell, ___ a well-known author, wrote an article ___ is about activism.

   a) who's / that b) whose / that c) who's / than d) whom / that

3. Gladwell's views, ___ he discusses in *The New Yorker*, are original and interesting.

   a) what b) wich c) who d) which

4. According to Gladwell, Facebook and Twitter are important ___, they do not have a significant impact on revolutions.

   a) , however b) , although c) ; however d) ; although

5. Gladwell argues that social networking forms "weak ties" between people ___ it does not convince people to engage in protest.

   a) because b) , so c) , which d) ; although

PART B

Underline and correct the errors in the following sentences.

EXAMPLE: I read an article <u>who</u> discusses violence. (that)

6. Americans can easily buy guns, Canadians must get special permits.

7. Last year, many violent riots around the world.

8. Gladwell suggests than it's easier to be heard in a social network, but harder for each voice to make a difference.

9. Sometimes protests become violent. Because opportunists take advantage of the chaos.

10. Leaders who treat citizens fairly are more likely to be valued, respected, and having support.

PART C

Complete the following embedded questions. Remember to change the position of the verb in the sentence, if necessary.

EXAMPLE: Where are we? Do you know where we are?

11. What is the problem? Do you know ______________________

12. Why did they protest? I wonder ______________________

13. Where are the police? Can you tell me ______________________

14. How have the police reacted? I don't know ______________________

15. When should we discuss it? I wonder ______________________

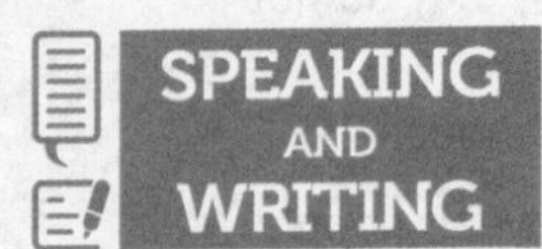

Letter to the Editor

Write a letter to the editor of a newspaper. Argue either that college tuition fees should increase or that they should not. Provide reasons for your opinion. Ensure that your letter has a variety of sentence types: simple, compound, and complex.

UNIT 11

Punctuation and Capitalization

Preview

IDENTIFY PUNCTUATION ERRORS

Work with a partner. Identify and correct twenty errors in capitalization or punctuation.

Every Summer, my friend's meet in Halifax, Nova Scotia. Last august, on a saturday morning; we went for a drive along Shore road. We walked along Mahone bay, and we could see the Atlantic ocean. Suddenly, we heard screams for help. A twenty-two-year old woman was shouting. She was in the water, and she could not get back to shore. Brad my brother in-law, had the presence of mind to do the following; take a rope from his car throw one end to the woman, and pull her to safety. Although, Brad had helped her, the woman was ungrateful. She was angry, "you should have jumped into the water to save me". Then she got into her car and drove away. We all agreed that she looked like a character from that television show called *Gossip girl*. Later, while we were driving to our hotel, Brad said: "I tried to do the right thing. She should'nt have been so ungrateful."

Punctuation: Forms and Usage

APOSTROPHES (')

Apostrophes in Contractions

Use an apostrophe to join a subject and a verb.

They**'re** popular. There**'s** a crowd outside the theatre.

Also use an apostrophe to join an auxiliary with *not*.

We ca**n't** see the show. There are**n't** any tickets left.

Apostrophes to Show Ownership

You can add an apostrophe followed by an –s ('s) to a noun to indicate possession.

Alicia is the child of Marco. She is Marco**'s** child.

If the noun is plural, put the apostrophe after the –s.

The boy**s'** clothes are in the washing machine.

If the noun has an irregular plural form, add –'s.

The men**'s** room is down the hall.

When two people have **joint ownership**, add the apostrophe to the second name. When two people have **separate ownership**, add apostrophes to both names.

Joint ownership: Marian and **Jake's** gallery is successful.
Separate ownership: **Marian's** and **Jake's** studios are in different buildings.

COLONS (:)

Use a colon

- after a complete sentence that introduces a list, or after the words *the following*;

  The play has the following parts**:** crime, punishment, and redemption.

- after a complete sentence that introduces a quotation;

  Picasso's advice was clear**:** "Find your passion."

- to introduce an explanation or example;

  The drama ended with a lesson**:** enjoy life.

- to separate the hours and minutes in expressions of time.

  The movie begins at 7**:**30 and ends at 10**:**00.

COMMAS (,)

Use a comma

- after an introductory word, phrase, or idea;

  First**,** Mrs. Rice closed her store.

  A few minutes later**,** she emptied the safe.

- to separate three or more words in a series (you can put a comma before the word *and*);

  The building is tall**,** old**,** and decrepit.

- around an interrupting phrase that gives additional information about the subject;

  Jenna**,** a student at Montmorency College**,** went through a traffic light.

- with a quotation, after an introductory phrase.

  She said**,** "The light was green."

ELLIPSES (. . .)

Use the ellipsis to show that you have omitted unnecessary information from a quotation. When you type the three periods, leave a space before and after each period.

Seligman wrote, "The path is very clear. . . . We must work together."

HYPHENS (-)

Use a hyphen

- when you spell out a compound number between 21 and 99;

  twenty-five   ninety-two   seventy-seven

- after some prefixes, such as *ex-*, *mid-*, and *self-*;

  ex-husband   mid-December   self-assured

- with some compound nouns (note that *compound* means "more than one part");

  mother-in-law   show-off   sister-in-law

- when you use a compound adjective before a noun. The compound adjective must express a single thought.

  one-way street   thirty-year-old woman   well-known actor

PERIODS (.)

Use a period at the end of a complete sentence and with the following titles: Ms., Mrs., Mr., and Dr. (Don't put a period after *Miss*.)

Mr. Fairhaven studied happiness and its effects on the brain.

QUOTATION MARKS (" ")

Use quotation marks around direct speech. Capitalize the first word in the quotation, and place end punctuation inside the closing quotation marks.

Oscar Wilde declared, **"A**ll art is useless**."**

Pradip asked, **"W**hat is the cost of that painting**?"**

SEMICOLONS (;)

Use a semicolon to join two independent and related clauses.

Gandhi was a pacifist; he believed in non-violence.

Capitalization: Forms and Usage

Always capitalize

- the pronoun *I* and the first word of every sentence;

  The man that **I** met is very nice.

- the days of the week, the months, and holidays;

  Friday   **J**une 8   **L**abour **D**ay

- the names of specific places, such as buildings, streets, parks, public squares, lakes, rivers, cities, provinces, and countries;

  Evan **A**venue   **L**ake **E**rie   **C**algary, **A**lberta

- the names of languages, nationalities, tribes, races, and religions;

  Spanish   **M**ohawk   **P**rotestant

- the titles of specific individuals;

  General **D**allaire | **P**rime **M**inister **L**ee | **M**rs. **P**eel

- the titles of specific school courses;

  Physics 201 | **E**nglish 101 | **B**eginner's **S**panish

- certain historical events, eras, and movements;

  World **W**ar **II** | **C**ubism | **G**roup of **S**even

- the important words in titles of literary or artistic works.

  ***O**n the **R**oad* | ***P**itch **P**erfect* | "**M**y **V**isit to **M**ontreal"

Practice

EXERCISE 1 APOSTROPHES

Write the possessive forms of the following phrases. To review apostrophe rules, see page 118.

EXAMPLE: the sister of the doctor ______ the doctor's sister ______

1. the brush of the artist ______
2. the brushes of the artists ______
3. the pictures of Sandra ______
4. the room of the child ______
5. the rooms of the children ______
6. the photo of Ross and Anna ______
7. the car of Ross and the car of Anna ______

COMMON APOSTROPHE ERRORS

Don't use an apostrophe before the final –s of a verb or a plural noun.

Mr. Garcia ~~want's~~ **wants** to open several ~~gallery's~~ **galleries**.

In negative contractions, remember that the apostrophe replaces the –*o* of the word *not*. Therefore, the apostrophe comes **after** the letter *n*.

He ~~does'nt~~ **doesn't** understand the problem.

EXERCISE 2 IDENTIFYING APOSTROPHE ERRORS

Underline and correct fifteen errors involving apostrophes and possessive forms. Note that you may need to add, remove, or move apostrophes. You also may need to add a final –s to words.

artist's
EXAMPLE: What is an artists motivation to create?

1. Many artist's paintings are unique. Have you ever heard of George Tooker? The American painters work earned him the National Medal of Honor in 2007. Several of his painting's have also appeared in New York galleries. Most art school's programs mention realist artists such as Tooker and Fernand Botero. In fact, Botero and Tooker's paintings hang in museums.

2. At first, George Tooker's parents did'nt like his choice of career. They wanted him to focus on literature. But he disobeyed his parents wishes and worked as an artist. His paintings are part of the movement known as magic realism. What makes his work unique is it's dark overtones. One of his most famous paintings is of a group of people trapped in a subway. Theyre gathered in a low-ceilinged subway car, incapable of escaping. Its a powerful and disturbing image.

3. Tooker's work was'nt popular during most of his life. In the recent past, most peoples' choice of favourite artist would not have been Tooker. However, now hes become a well-known realist painter and is known for making mundane situations seem ominous or threatening. His despondent view of the modern world has influenced contemporary artists. Youll find his artwork in many art gallery's collections.

SPECIAL COMMA RULES

Commas with *Who*, *Which*, and *That*

Review the comma rules in clauses beginning with *who*, *which*, or *that*.

- ***Which***

  Always use commas to set off clauses beginning with *which*.

  The brain, **which** is a complex organ, develops rapidly.

- ***That***

  Don't use commas to set off clauses beginning with *that*.

  The house **that** I grew up in was demolished last year.

→

- ***Who***

When a clause begins with *who*, you may or may not need a comma. If the clause contains **non-essential** information, put commas around it. If the clause is **essential** to the meaning of the sentence, it does not require commas.

Essential: Many people <u>who have brain injuries</u> undergo subtle personality changes.
(The underlined clause is essential to understand the meaning of the sentence.)

Non-essential: Dr. Jay Geidd, <u>**who** lives in Maryland,</u> made an important discovery.
(The underlined clause contains extra information, but if you removed the clause, the sentence would still have a clear meaning.)

Commas with Dependent Clauses

If a sentence begins with a dependent clause (a clause beginning with a subordinator such as *although* or *because*), place a comma after it. However, if the dependent clause appears in the middle of the sentence, no comma is necessary. Notice the difference in the next two sentences.

Comma: <u>Because rents are so high</u>, some young adults live with their parents.

No comma: Some adults live with their parents <u>because rents are so high</u>.

TIP

Comma Error

Don't separate the main subject and verb with a comma.

The researcher, was surprised with the results of the experiment.

EXERCISE 3 EDITING FOR COMMAS

Correct twelve comma errors by adding or removing commas, as appropriate.

EXAMPLE: Susanna Moodie, who was born in England, became one of Canada's most renowned authors.

1. In *Roughing It in the Bush* Susanna Moodie wrote about living on a Canadian farm in the 1830s. Moodie who enjoyed luxuries did not enjoy life in the wild. At the same time, she was not a snob. People in different social classes, in Moodie's opinion are separated only by the quality of their education.

Margaret Atwood

2. Moodie who enjoyed writing, was asked to create a guide for immigrants from Britain. In her journals, she told British citizens what to expect, when they arrived in Canada. Her anecdotes which were filled with fascinating details described the beauty and misery in Canada. She was also capable of humour. She said "I have no wish for a second husband. I had enough of the first."

3. In the 1970s, Moodie's work increased in popularity, because Margaret Atwood wrote poems about Moodie. Atwood, who was born more than a hundred years after Moodie had written several bestselling novels. In Atwood's view Moodie is one of the greatest writers in Canadian history.

HYPHENS

Remember to use a hyphen when a compound adjective appears before a noun. The compound adjective must express a single thought.

The department has a <u>two-way</u> mirror.
Detectives interviewed a <u>twenty-year-old</u> man.

Note: There is no hyphen if the compound adjective is after the noun. In addition, if the adjectives before a noun function independently, don't add a hyphen.

The man is twenty years old.	(The compound adjective is after the noun.)
Lange was a motivated, creative woman.	(The two adjectives function separately.)

TIP

Non-Hyphenated Compound Adjectives

Some compound adjectives never take a hyphen, even when they appear before a noun.

World Wide Web   health food store   real estate agent

EXERCISE 4 **ADDING PUNCTUATION**

Add twenty missing punctuation marks to the following paragraphs. When necessary, add a period, comma, colon, semicolon, hyphen, or apostrophe. You can review the information about punctuation on page 118.

EXAMPLE: The graphic novel, which is very old, is about teen heroes.

1. My brother in law loves manga illustrations. The name *manga* which means "whimsical drawings," defines a genre of animation. There are two popular forms of manga Shonen manga for men and Shojo manga for women. At the end of World War II Japanese manga comics were introduced to North America. After soldiers completed their tours of duty many of them brought the comics back to the US.

2. Early manga, which was mostly aimed at fifteen-year old boys focused on adventure stories. For example the comics dealt with robots, space travel, and action heroes. When womens manga first appeared it was produced by men. However, in recent decades, most Shojo manga has been created by women. For example, Mrs Rumiko Takahashi is one of Japans wealthiest artists she has sold over 170 million comics. When the self assured artist first began her career, she worked with the following black pens, felt markers, and white paper.

→

3. According to the magazine *Publishers Weekly* the manga market in North America is now worth roughly $175 million. Many manga comics have content that may be sexually explicit violent, or generally dark thus, not everyone likes them. However, in comparison to other types of entertainment manga is reasonably tame.

QUOTATIONS

Review the following details about how to punctuate quotations.

Opening Phrase or Sentence

In quotations, put a comma after the opening phrase. Put a colon after the opening sentence.

Comma: Pablo Picasso said, "Art is a lie that makes us realize the truth."
Colon: The critic was shocked: "What is Picasso doing?"

Interrupting Phrase

When a quotation is interrupted, place a comma after the first part of the quotation, and place another comma after the interrupting phrase.

"In the end," says dancer Martha Graham, "it all comes down to breathing."

Ending Phrase

When you place a phrase at the end of a quotation, end the quotation with a comma instead of a period.

"Great art picks up where nature ends," said Marc Chagall.

If your quotation ends with other punctuation, put it inside the quotation mark.

"Who is the greatest painter**?**" the student asked.
"That question cannot be answered**!**" the curator replied.

Integrated Quotation

If a quotation isn't a complete sentence, and you simply integrate it into your sentence, don't capitalize the first word of the quotation.

Dorothy Nixon calls herself a "**t**errible mother."

Quotations Inside Quotations

If one quotation is inside another quotation, then use single quotation marks (' ') around the inside quotation.

The young sailor was furious: "He was foaming with passion at the barbarous indifference manifested by the men in the boat. He said, 'If they had given me the oar in time, I could have saved him.'"

Page Numbers

Put the page number in parentheses. Place the final period after the parentheses. (Your teacher may ask you to indicate the paragraph number instead of the page number.)

Jan Wong wrote, "In July 1973, I prepared to leave China" **(122).**

EXERCISE 5 **QUOTATIONS**

In each sentence, the quotation is set in bold. Add capital letters, quotation marks, commas, or colons to the quotations, as necessary.

EXAMPLE: Professor Wayne Johnson asks **where are the great female artists?**

1. Famous music producer Rick Rubin says **right now, if you listen to pop, everything is in perfect pitch, perfect time, and perfect tune**
2. **Auto-Tune was originally created to fix pitch and tone problems in singers' voices** according to Anna Pulley.
3. **The Auto-Tune effect just worked for my voice** proclaimed rapper T-Pain.
4. **I know Auto-Tune better than anyone** said T-Pain **and even I'm just figuring out all the ways you can use it to change the mood of a record**
5. *Time* journalist Josh Tyrangiel says that technology **can transform a wavering performance into something technically flawless**
6. **It makes singers sound too perfect** says music lover Andrea Berezan **and perfect singing is boring**
7. Canadian recording artist Neko Case shows her contempt for Auto-Tune **when I hear Auto-Tune on somebody's voice, I don't take him seriously** (16)
8. **Too many pop stars also lip-synch in concert** declares Jay Segal.
9. Neil McCormack mentions an incident at a live show **I saw Madonna drop her microphone, and it didn't affect her performance** (28)
10. Music fan Chelsea Oberman says **When I pay $80 to see a live concert, and the singer lip-synchs, I sometimes shout use your voice.**

CAPITALIZATION

Most capitalization rules apply to specific individuals, places, and school courses. If you make a general reference without giving a specific name, capitalization is unnecessary.

She lives on a nice street. It's called **K**elvin **A**venue.

EXERCISE 6 **CAPITALIZATION**

Add twenty missing capital letters to the following paragraphs. To review capitalization rules, see page 119.

EXAMPLE: Miku's best song is "~~l~~ove ~~i~~s ~~w~~ar." (L I W)

1. Hatsune Miku, with her turquoise pigtails and her sweet voice, has become a star in Asia. The article "Virtual Singer tops the charts" on *Web Japan* describes Miku: "She is no girl at all." Hatsune Miku is actually an artificial voice accompanied by a virtual avatar.

2. The british fashion magazine *Clash* featured Miku's virtual character on the cover of its fifty-ninth issue. The character has also appeared in the manga magazine *Comic rush*. Miku's voice is the result of a voice-synthesizing software program. It uses an audio library of samples from japanese voice actress Fujita Saki to create new, synthesized songs. In the article "Pixel perfect," Karley Sciortino describes the world of Miku. For under $200, aspiring songwriters buy the software program and then write songs for the virtual singer.

3. Crypton future media has made a lot of money from Miku. In 2007, Miku was the top-selling computer program in Japan. In april 2010, an updated version was released. In the newspaper *Los Angeles times*, journalist Tiffany Hsu wrote, "the virtual diva's albums have topped the Japanese charts." The character Miku also advertises products and has been a spokesperson for the Good Smile racing Company. Thousands of fans show up to Miku concerts. In august of 2009, at her first concert, Miku was projected to the audience as a giant 3-D hologram. There were Japanese, korean, and Chinese fans at the show. Some fans were buddhists and others were not. In july 2011, she performed at the Los Angeles convention Center, at 1201 South Figueroa street. Many students went to the show. Kylie Moreau, a student at Centennial high school, loved watching the hologram. Could Miku change the way music is produced?

PUNCTUATING TITLES

Place the title of a short work (such as a magazine article) in quotation marks. Italicize the title of a longer document (or underline titles in handwritten documents). Capitalize the first word and all major words in titles. It's not necessary to capitalize prepositions and articles.

	Short Work		**Long Work**
short story:	"The Lottery"	**book:**	*The Grapes of Wrath*
Web article:	"Music Artists Lose Out"	**website:**	*CBCNews*
newspaper article:	"Early Accomplishments"	**newspaper:**	*The Calgary Herald*
magazine article:	"The City's Hottest Ticket"	**magazine:**	*Rolling Stone*
essay:	"Hip-Hop Nation"	**textbook:**	*Common Culture*
TV episode:	"The Search Party"	**TV series:**	*Game of Thrones*
song:	"Mouths to Feed"	**CD:**	*Release Therapy*
poem:	"Howl"	**movie:**	*Man of Steel*

EXERCISE 7 **TITLE PUNCTUATION**

Add ten missing capital letters and punctuate seven titles. Add quotation marks where appropriate and underline titles that should normally be italicized.

In 2005, Terry Fallis hunted for a publisher for his book called The Best laid plans. His novel is about an ottawa politician who, despite his distaste for the political scene, is elected to canada's Parliament. When no publishers were interested, Fallis published his book by himself. Amazingly, his podcasts of book excerpts became popular. Then he won some literary awards. For example, he won the Canada Reads contest on february 9, 2011. His book beat Ami McKay's popular novel, The Birth house. In a newspaper interview with the Toronto star, in the column called afterword, Fallis said that a major publishing company would publish his novel for a mass audience. Since then, Fallis has published his second book, The High road. Grant Black, a reporter for The Globe and Mail, reviewed Fallis's second novel. In his article A Missed opportunity, Black wrote that the book "didn't deliver."

EXERCISE 8 **IDENTIFYING PUNCTUATION ERRORS**

Correct the errors involving punctuation or capitalization in the following sentences. Add underlines to titles that should be in italics. The number of errors in each sentence is indicated in brackets.

EXAMPLE: [1] Marcel Dzama, a well known artist, does watercolour paintings.

1. [5] Last january, my brother was accepted into the Academy of fine arts on wellington street.

2. [6] He said "Did you see the article about creativity called "The left brain" in the Vancouver sun newspaper"?

3. [2] My father in law is a huge fan of Marcel Dzama's artwork.

4. [5] When Dzama was a twenty-one year old art student at the university of Winnipeg he helped start the renowned Royal art Lodge.

5. [3] In 2005 Dzama drew the album cover for Beck's record *Guero* he has also illustrated Nick Hornby's essay collection called Songbook.

6. [3] Many of Dzamas paintings feature the same elements nightmarish comic landscapes modern nostalgia, and bats.

7. [2] One of his most famous works a diorama of riflemen shooting down bats, birds, and severed heads shows Dzama's darkly comic sensibilities.

8. [4] Dzama described the meaning of his diorama "They're shooting the character's I decided I would'nt be drawing anymore".

9. [4] His artwork which has been exhibited at New York's museum of modern Art is popular among celebrities such as Jim Carrey.

10. [4] A best selling art book of Dzama's work, The Berlin years, was released in 2003, and Dzama co authored several other art collections.

11. [3] Adam Clay loves art "My mother always says, Art feeds the soul. "

12. [3] Adam, who speaks french puts art in his apartment near the Rideau canal.

UNIT Review

Add punctuation to the following sentences. If you don't know an answer, go back and review the appropriate section. Also underline three titles that should normally be italicized.

1. Most human's believe in life after death they want to believe that life has meaning.
2. My mother always says don't believe everything that you read.
3. Last month, I read the following The war of the worlds, 1984, and Animal farm.
4. In december, they celebrated thirty five years of marriage.
5. I read an article in The Boston Globe called The final shift.

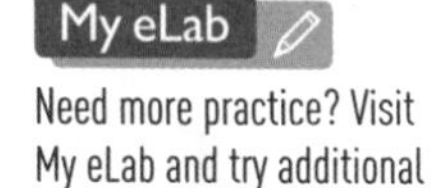

Need more practice? Visit My eLab and try additional grammar exercises.

Final Review

PART A

For each of the sentences, circle the letter of the answer that best fills in the blank. Note that *X* means "nothing."

1. Some people perform acts of kindness, including ___ donating time, money, and publicity to charities.
   a) ;　　b) :　　c) X
2. For the Diabetes Association, Alana donated the following ___ clothing, jewellery, and money.
   a) ;　　b) :　　c) X
3. She is self-sufficient ___ "I pay my own expenses ___
   a) : / "!　　b) , / !"　　c) : / !"
4. She loved the novel called ___
   a) "The Hunger Games"
   b) *The Hunger Games*
   c) *The hunger games*
5. The artist Paul Gauguin said ___ "Art is either plagiarism or revolution ___
   a) , / " (10).　　b) : / ." (10)　　c) : / " (10).

PART B

Identify five titles. Add quotation marks where appropriate and underline titles that should normally be italicized. Also correct fifteen other errors involving punctuation or capitalization.

6. Last september, an interesting article appeared in the Toronto Star. The article, called The art of Rewiring a Brain, describes artist John Newmans recovery from a stroke using art therapy. A journalist for the magazine Health News Digest also discusses the therapy.

7. In 2006, Newman's stroke took his lifes passion away from him he could no longer paint with his right hand. However, Newman taught himself to paint with his left hand. According to Newman, it was hard work, "I didn't have any control over my left hand." By the age of seventy eight, Newman's new artwork was again displayed in a prominent Toronto gallery. The exhibit lasted until friday, October 8.

8. Newman, a former professor at the Ontario College of Art and design believes that his brain made new connections when he constantly drew with his left hand. He thinks that other patient's can also use art therapy to help rebuild their brains.

9. An article in the Deccan herald entitled Healing Through Art showed that art therapy can also be useful for young people with emotional or psychological problems. Robert Allen, a visual art therapist, said: "it is a terrific diagnosis tool".

Playing Paparazzi

Working with a partner, imagine a discussion between two well-known celebrities. Write ten lines of dialogue. Use quotation marks around direct speech.

UNIT 12

Spelling and Word Choice

Preview

DICTATION

Your teacher will read nine sentences out loud. Write each of the sentences.

1. ______________________________

2. ______________________________

3. ______________________________

4. ______________________________

5. ______________________________

6. ______________________________

7. ______________________________

8. ______________________________

9. ______________________________

Spelling: Forms and Usage

Spelling correctly is important. According to the Canadian Broadcasting Corporation, one spelling mistake on a commercial website can cut sales by half. Review the following spelling rules to help you become a better speller.

WRITING *–GHT* AND *–GTH*

The past forms of many verbs end in ***–ght***. In such words, the *–gh* is silent. Thus, *thought* is pronounced *thot*.

bou**ght** | cau**ght**

Other words end in ***–gth***. When you pronounce the following words, ensure that you pronounce the final *–th* by pushing your tongue slightly between your upper and lower front teeth.

stren**gth** | len**gth**

WRITING *–IE* OR *–EI*

To learn the spelling of words containing ***–ie*** or ***–ei***, remember the following rhyme. Write *–i* before *–e*, except after *–c*, or when *–ei* is pronounced as *ay*, as in *neighbour* and *weigh*.

–*i* before –*e*:	bel**ie**ve	f**ie**ld
–*ei* after –*c*:	rec**ei**ve	c**ei**ling
–*ei* pronounced as *ay*:	w**ei**gh	v**ei**n

Note: There are several exceptions to the above rule.

anc**ie**nt	for**ei**gn	l**ei**sure	sc**ie**nce	soc**ie**ty
either	h**ei**ght	n**ei**ther	s**ei**ze	w**ei**rd

ADDING PREFIXES AND SUFFIXES

A **prefix** is added to the beginning of a word, and it changes the word's meaning. When you add a prefix to a word, the last letter of the prefix and the first letter of the main word can be the same; keep both. Some common prefixes include *dis-*, *il-*, *im-*, *in-*, *mis-*, *non-*, and *re-*.

u**n** + **n**atural = u**nn**atural | mi**s** + **s**pell = mi**ss**pell

When you add a **suffix** to the end of a word, it changes the word's tense and/or meaning. When you add the suffix *–ly* to a root word that ends in *–l*, keep the *–l* of the root word. The new word will have two *–l*s. If the root word ends in *–e*, keep the *–e*.

fina**l** + **l**y = fina**ll**y | sur**e** + **ly** = sur**ely**

COMMONLY MISSPELLED WORDS

The following are some commonly misspelled words.

Note: A more complete list appears in *Avenues 3: Grammar Review Guide*.

address	embarrassed	government
aggressive	environment	heroes
apartment	exaggerated	human
bankrupt	example	interesting
committed	family	medicine
developed	future	ninth

➜

payment
personality
possess
potential
questioned
recommend
recommendation
responsibility
responsible
succeed
successful
tomorrow

Word Choice: Forms and Usage

The following sets of words sound alike but have very different meanings.

SOME COMMONLY CONFUSED WORDS

WORD	MEANING	USAGE
accept **except**	to receive; to admit excluding; other than	You should really **accept** my apology. Everyone **except** Lauren was at the movie.
allowed **aloud**	permitted spoken audibly	The children aren't **allowed** to stay up past nine. We couldn't speak **aloud**, so we whispered.
considerate **considered**	kind and understanding contemplated; regarded as	His lawyer was a very gentle and **considerate** person. He was **considered** the main suspect in the case.
hole **whole**	an opening in something the full amount	There is a large **hole** where the house used to be. The company tore down the **whole** house.
independence **independent**	the state of being free from control not controlled by others	India celebrated fifty years of **independence**. Katia is **independent**. She pays her own bills.
loose **lose** **loss** **lost**	not tight; baggy to misplace something a decrease in value misplaced or unable to be found; unable to find one's way (past form of *lose*)	My pants are too **loose**. I need a belt. I often **lose** my keys. The company suffered a **loss** for the third year in a row. We didn't know how to get to the new store, and instead we got **lost**.
price **prize**	the cost of something a reward for winning a contest	The sofa is on sale for a very good **price**. He won the contest, and his **prize** was a trip to Hawaii.
quiet **quit** **quite**	silent to discontinue a job or habit to a considerable degree	It is very **quiet** outside. There are no sounds. Marco **quit** smoking. He also **quit** his job. The politician is **quite** young. He's just twenty years old.
sale **sell**	a reduced price to transfer something in exchange for money	The tires were on **sale** for fifty percent off. The new hardware store **sells** tires.
steal **still**	to take without permission remaining in place; a past situation continues to exist	The thief tried to **steal** my car. The thief is sitting very **still** in his cell. He is **still** in police custody.

Practice

EXERCISE 1 **IDENTIFY SPELLING ERRORS**

Underline and correct sixteen spelling mistakes in the following paragraphs. You could review the list of commonly misspelled words on pages 132–133.

EXAMPLE: People want a better world so they <u>figth</u> (fight) for justice.

1. For a democracy to suceed, citizens must be able to speak freely about issues. A SLAPP, or strategic lawsuit against public participation, permits someone to act in an agressive manner toward critics. Unfortunatly, private citizens have very little protection against such lawsuits.

2. Often, SLAPP cases relate to the enviroment. For exemple, in 2004, Serge Galipeau and Christine Landry complained about the strong odours from a nearby dump. They couldn't leave the windows of their appartement open because they developped headaches. The dump's owners, who were embarased by the publicity, brought a $1.25 million defamation lawsuit against the couple. Any business owner with a deceitful personnality may exagerrate the damage to the company's reputation. However, it is unnethical to allow companies to silence consumers.

3. To discourage any futur SLAPPs, some governments have introduced anti-SLAPP legislation. For example, Quebec and Pennsylvania have such laws. Hopefully, companies will take responsability for their mistakes instead of attacking critics. However, many people have questionned the effectiveness of anti-SLAPP legislation. Meanwhile, many victims of SLAPPs spend a lot of time and money defending themselves. They are not always successfull. Still, most whistle-blowers recommand that people fight for justice.

SPELLING TWO-PART WORDS

Some indefinite pronouns sound as if they should be two separate words, but they are only one.

- **Words with *any*:** anything, anyone, anybody, anywhere
- **Words *with some*:** something, someone, somebody, somewhere
- **Words with *every*:** everything, everyone, everybody, everywhere

Another* and *A lot

Another is always one word. Bonnie committed **another** crime.

A lot is always two words. She robbed **a lot** of banks.

TIP

Words Ending in *–ful*

Although the word *full* ends in two *–ls*, when *full* is added to another word as a suffix, it ends in only one *–l*.

beautifu**l** peacefu**l** wonderfu**l**

Exception: Notice the unusual spelling when *full* and *fill* are combined: *fulfill*.

Note: When you add the suffix *–ly*, the final word has two *–ls*.

beautifu**ll**y peacefu**ll**y wonderfu**ll**y

EXERCISE 2 **IDENTIFY SPELLING ERRORS**

Underline and correct fifteen spelling mistakes.

Another
EXAMPLE: An other scandal occurred last year.

1. Many good people enter politics because they believe it is a fullfilling job. They are truthfull, and they have the personal strenght to avoid making imoral choices. However, not all politicians are honest. Some times they accept bribes. Alot of political leaders have definitly been involved in scandals. In 1995, Canadian Prime Minister Brian Mulroney was accused of accepting a $225,000 cash paiement placed in an envelope, but he said it was for work he had done.

2. In addition, during Canada's 2011 election, some body orchestrated "robocalls" to voters, telling them to go to an other polling station. Voters turned up at the new locations and realized that the calls had been a hoax. →

Often, when they finaly made it to the real polling stations, they were too late and couldn't vote. No body knows who organized the calls. Often, citizens discover that their heros, especially in the governement, are capable of just about any thing.

STANDARD ENGLISH

In both academic and professional writing, you should use standard English. The word *standard* doesn't imply "better." Standard English is the common language generally used and expected in schools, businesses, and government institutions.

Avoid Slang

Slang is non-standard language that is used in informal situations. In academic writing, it is preferable to use more formal terms. Review the following examples of slang.

cool guy dude kid psyched stuff

Slang: The kid was psyched.
Better: The **child** was **excited**.

TIP

Changing Slang

Slang changes over time, and it also differs depending on generational and regional influences. For example, in the past, people used the words *swell* or *groovy* to show admiration. More recent terms are *awesome*, *cool*, and *sick*. In fact, very soon, some of this book's examples might be considered "lame."

EXERCISE 3 **IDENTIFY SLANG**

Underline and correct ten examples of slang. Replace each slang term with a standard English word.

EXAMPLE: The old dude [man] was really surprised.

1. Philip Zimbardo, a psychology professor, wanted to determine if roles make people behave badly. In the Stanford Prison Experiment, some regular guys agreed to play the role of prisoners, and others played the role of prison guards. The prisoners weren't allowed to bring any of their personal stuff into the simulated prison.

2. Originally, Zimbardo thought the guards would show some TLC to the prisoners, but he was really shocked when some of the guards started acting like total jerks. They did some bad stuff to the prisoners.

3. One of the guards, for instance, was totally not cool. He became full of it, and he started making rules that were dumb. The men who were the prisoners became really whipped. A few of them freaked and left the experiment early.

TIP

Rob and *Steal*

Both ***rob*** and ***steal*** mean "to take property illegally." However, *to steal* is to take an entire object. *To rob* is to take something from the object or to take something from someone. Notice the difference in meaning.

He **robbed** the car.	He took valuables, such as the GPS device, from the car.
He **robbed** me.	He took something from me.
He **stole** the car.	He took the car.

EXERCISE 4 **WORD CHOICE**

Underline the appropriate word in parentheses. If you are not sure of your answer, review the list of commonly confused words on page 133.

EXAMPLE: What have you got to (loose / lose)? Take a chance!

1. In my family, everyone (accept / except) my mother is interested in politics. We have spent (hole / whole) weekends debating issues. My father hates to (loose / loss / lose) the debates, so he uses persuasive tactics to convince us that he is right. He is never at a (lose / loss / lost) for words. My mother, on the other hand, remains (quit / quite / quiet). During our discussions, we are (considered / considerate) to each other. For instance, last weekend, we discussed non-violent revolutions. Five days later, we are (steal / still) discussing the topic.

2. Most people (accept / except) that non-violent revolution is possible. In fact, non-violent resistance has (aloud / allowed) many nations to emerge from authoritarianism. For example, the Singing Revolution in Eastern Europe led to Estonia, Latvia, and Lithuania gaining (independents / independence). Even →

better, those countries won their freedom without paying a heavy (prize / price) in lives (loss / lost). During the Singing Revolution, hundreds of thousands of people sang their national anthems, which was a right they had (lose / lost / loss) during Soviet rule. They were really (quit / quite / quiet) brave, because they often faced Soviet tanks. They were tired of Soviet authorities (stealing / robbing) them. After four years of civil disobedience, those countries finally won the (prize / price) of freedom, in 1991.

3. Democratic governments can help people who are living under dictatorships. For instance, trade embargoes have been effective. Often, a group of countries refuses to (sale / sell) weapons to the authoritarian regime. People in privileged nations should be (considered / considerate) and try to help where they can. For example, 2010 saw the growth of the "Arab Spring." Many people (considered / considerate) certain Middle Eastern dictators untouchable just a few short years ago, but people in Tunisia and Egypt have proven the power of non-violent resistance.

MORE COMMONLY CONFUSED WORDS

Some English words may look like words in your own language. However, their meaning in English may not match their meaning in your language. Memorize the following words and their meanings.

Learn* and *Teach

A person discovering information ***learns***. A person providing information ***teaches***.

He **learned** how to read when he was five.
His mother **taught** him how to read.

Memory*, *Remind*, *Remember*, and *Souvenir

Memory is a noun meaning "the capacity to retain past impressions." ***Remind*** is a verb meaning "to cause a person to remember something." ***Remember*** is a verb meaning "to recall." A ***souvenir*** is a memento that you buy to remind yourself of a special place.

When we went to New York, we brought back a **souvenir** of the Statue of Liberty. I **remember** many details about our trip. Please **remind** me to call my grandmother and tell her about it. She is eighty, but she has a great **memory**.

Say* and *Tell

Use ***say*** in direct and indirect quotations. Follow *say* with the actual words that were said. ***Tell*** is followed by a noun or pronoun. You must tell somebody something.

Alex **said**, "Let's move to Nova Scotia."
He **told** me that he wanted to move to Halifax.

TIP

Quit

You do not quit a person or place, you leave it.

He ~~quit~~ **left** the country last month.

EXERCISE 5 MORE WORD CHOICE

Underline and correct one error involving commonly confused words in each of the sentences below. Write *C* beside the sentences that are correct.

1. Some soldiers loose the ability to cope with everyday life after they leave the battlefield. ______ A psychology professor learned me about the symptoms and effects of post-traumatic stress disorder (PTSD). ______ He said me that soldiers in war zones are especially susceptible to developing PTSD. ______ About 12 percent of veterans develop the disorder after they are exposed to high-risk combat situations. ______ For instance, my professor said that if I spent a hole year on the front lines in Iraq, I would have a chance of developing it. ______

2. For many soldiers, quitting a war zone and returning home is traumatic. ______ Often, family members feel like the PTSD has stolen them of the person they used to know. ______ For instance, some veterans from the Afghanistan conflict aloud psychologists to question them. ______ The former soldiers said that certain events can remember them of their war experiences, a phenomenon known as "flashbacks." ______ Even thirty years later, many retain painful souvenirs of the war. ______ Some soldiers loose their moral balance. ______ For example, a veteran living in New York shot a neighbour because he thought the man was an intruder. ______ He said, "I thought he stole me and was going to take my computer!" ______

3. Studies on soldiers should learn us about the importance of providing psychological assistance to those returning from combat. ______ It's important not to glorify wars or diminish the impact they have on the soldiers who fight them. ______ It was Oscar Wilde who told, "As long as war is regarded as wicked, it will always have its fascination. ______ When it is looked upon as vulgar, it will cease to be popular." ______

PREPOSITIONAL EXPRESSIONS

Some words are followed by certain prepositions. Memorize the following **prepositional expressions** and the two examples of their usage. A more complete list of prepositional expressions appears in your *Avenues 3: Grammar Review Guide*.

apologize for	consist of	look at	responsible for
ask for	depend on	participate in	scared of
believe in	insist on	prepared for	search for
capable of	interested in	rely on	specialize in

Toni was responsible **for** the accident.

They depend **on** science to answer difficult questions.

EXERCISE 6 **PREPOSITIONAL EXPRESSIONS**

Fill in the blanks with appropriate prepositions to complete the prepositional expressions.

EXAMPLE: My father really depends on my mother.

1. In times of need, can we depend ____________ others to help us? A part of the brain, called the limbic system, is responsible ____________ our emotional reactions. In the past, some scientists believed that humans were not capable ____________ altruistic behaviour until they were properly socialized and their brains were fairly developed. However, some intriguing studies suggest that helpful behaviour begins at a very early age.

2. Felix Warneken and Mike Tomasello are researchers who specialize ____________ human behaviour, and they are interested ____________ altruism. They developed scenarios in which an adult wasn't capable ____________ solving a simple problem. Some very young children participated ____________ the experiments. In one study, Warneken hung clothing on a line and then dropped a peg that was out of his reach while a baby played nearby. He looked ____________ the baby, but he didn't ask ____________ help. Over 80 percent of the time, the baby would pick up the peg and hand it to him.

3. In another version of the experiment, Warneken threw the peg on the ground. In those tests, the babies appeared to be scared ____________ him, and they didn't pick up the item. The babies helped Warneken only when they knew that he needed help to complete his goal of hanging the clothes.

4. The experiments indicate that infants, who have very little socialization or language skills, are willing to help others. They feel responsible __________ the well-being of people around them. Such studies help explain why human beings can rely __________ each other in times of need.

UNIT Review

Complete the following exercises. If you don't know an answer, go back and review the appropriate section.

1. Underline the correctly spelled words in the pairs below.
   - a) nineth / ninth
   - b) fulfil / fulfill
   - c) naturally / naturaly
   - d) adress / address
   - e) responsible / responsable
   - f) government /governement
2. Underline and correct the word-usage errors in the sentences below.
   - a) You might win a price if you buy a ticket for the contest.
   - b) My coach said me to work harder.
   - c) I need to sale some of my old hockey equipment.
   - d) Tony is responsible of the boy's death.

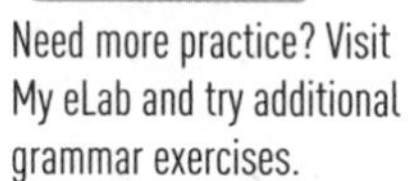

Final Review

PART A

Correct all misspelled words from the following list. Write *C* next to the words that are spelled correctly.

EXAMPLE: shure sure

1.	unusualy	________	**7.**	recommand	________
2.	writting	________	**8.**	another	________
3.	exaggerated	________	**9.**	alot	________
4.	personnality	________	**10.**	questionning	________
5.	responsability	________	**11.**	definitly	________
6.	strenght	________	**12.**	finally	________

PART B

Underline and correct eight errors involving word choice.

EXAMPLE: My father <u>learned</u> (taught) me about the case.

13. What moves people to action? Recently, somebody remembered me of an article by Nicholas Kristof called "What Moves Us." He explains that good people aren't moved by news about genocide and famine. However, if someone looses a child or a puppy, humans react. In one experiment, psychologists asked people to give $5 to charity. They were aloud to choose who would get the money: a seven-year-old girl or 21 million Africans. For most participants, the young girl was considerate the most deserving of the money. Kristof tells, "Evidence is overwhelming that humans respond to the suffering of individuals rather than groups."

14. If we except the research, what does this mean for charities? If an animal shelter wants to sale charity tickets to raise money, it should mention a specific dog in its publicity. Perhaps Kristof should learn aid organizations about the study.

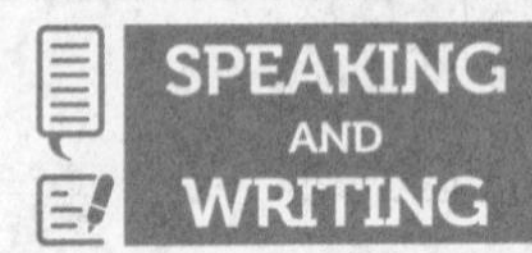

Identify Your Misspelled Words

Working with a partner, review the commonly misspelled words in your *Avenues 3: Grammar Review Guide*. Using your partner's booklet, quiz him or her on words. Underline or highlight every word that your partner misspells. Then give your review guide to your partner, and he or she will quiz you.

When you finish, construct a paragraph using some of the words that you commonly misspell.

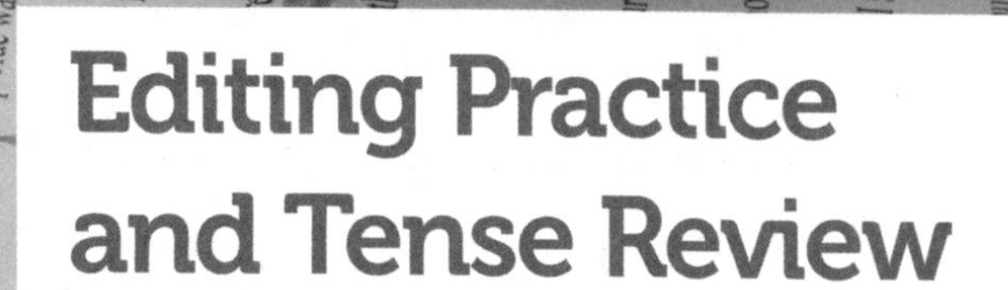

Editing Practice and Tense Review

Practise editing student writing. The following exercises contain a variety of errors.

EXERCISE 1 **EDITING**

Correct twenty-five errors in this student essay, not including the example. An editing symbol appears above each error. To understand the meaning of each symbol, look at the "Guide for Correcting Writing Errors" on the inside back cover of this book.

1. What is ~~the~~ (X) the beauty? Some people think that (WC) you need a perfect body. They are (WF) influence by the media and the photos of famous people who are beautiful. But (PL) that celebrities sometimes have surgery to look perfect. In addition, photographers retouch pictures of famous people. (SP) Unfortunatly, people take dangerous risks to attain a beauty ideal.

2. First, some people (VT) are not eating very much and it affects (WC) her health. For (SP) exemple, my friend (DS) she (VT) is always trying to (WC) loose weight, and she doesn't look (X) like very good. Last year, she (VT) was going to the hospital three times. We worried about her. Today, she still has an eating disorder.

3. Men also do horrible thing (PL) to be perfect in the eyes of society. One of the biggest problem (PL) for men is steroids. Those drug (PL) are easy to get. Steroids can cause many problems for men's healt (SP). Sometimes, men also are exercising (VT) for hours each day. Because they want to be muscular (F). My friend, who speaks spanish (C), goes to the gym every day. He thinks his muscles will impress women. But sometimes he pushes hisself (SP) too much. Since last April, he has (VT) many problems wiht (SP) his knees.

4. Every day, people do dangerous things to look perfect. Instead, they should try to enjoy life and not worry about their appearance. What will be the beauty ideal (WO) in the futur (SP)? Maybe women of average size and men with very little muscle development will be considerate (WC) perfect.

EXERCISE 2 **EDITING**

Correct twenty errors in the following student paragraph. An editing symbol appears above each error. To understand the meaning of each symbol, look at the "Guide for Correcting Writing Errors" on the inside back cover of this book.

Almost everyone has experimented (WC) the magic of litterature (SP). Writers share personal point (PL) of view. Essays and stories make us thinking (WF) about issues in our society. Additionaly (SP), most of us enjoy to hear (WF) about the past. For example, in the text "My visit (C) to Montreal," Susanna Moodie tells ⌃ (Ω) about that canadian (C) city in the 1830s. Her story helps us understands (WF) what was she (WO) feeling at that time. Her

SV RO
impressions of Montreal was mixed, she thought that the scenery was beautiful,

PL //
the persons were friendly, and there were dirty streets. She describes the smells

P P
in the city, "The air was loaded with intolerable vapours". (119) She also tells

WC
a story about a man which drowned because bystanders didn't help him. She

X
questions why do people ignore others who are in distress. Definitely, reading

can teach us about an other time and place.

EXERCISE 3 TENSE PROBLEMS

Underline and correct fifteen errors. Look for problems with verb tense and spelling, as well as errors with modals and conditional forms.

1. In 2006, Microsoft dominated the personal-computer market. To get a larger market share, Apple launched a clever ad campaign. The "Get a Mac" campaign has lasted from 2006 to 2010. In each ad, a young, hip guy will say, "I'm a Mac." An older man in a suit would replied, "I'm a PC." Each commercial had a little story. For example, in the first commercial, the PC complained about the viruses that could affect him. The Mac quietly mentionned that he did not get viruses. In every ad, the PC will get agitated, and the Mac would remaining calm.

2. The ads were extremely successful, but they also made Bill Gates feeling quite angry. Perhaps if Microsoft would have spent more money on better advertising, it could have responded effectively. At that time, most consumers can see the humour in the ads, and they laught at Microsoft. The ads were very effective. In fact, since the ads first aired, many consumers switched from PC computers to Apple computers. However, back in 2006, some consumers thougth that the commercials was unfair. That year, in an article for *Slate* magazine, Seth Stevenson has wrote that the ads were "mean-spirited."

EXERCISE 4 EDITING

Underline and correct twenty grammar errors.

1. Memory plays an important role in ours lives. But would the ability to remember every detail being useful? Actress Marilu Henner has a condition called "highly superior autobiographical memory." During her childhood, she has discovered that she could remember details about each days. If Henner would have become a professor or other academic, she probably would of realized the rarity of her condition. Certainly, her amazing memory has been very helpful in her career as an actress.

2. Next month, I'm gonna get married to a man named Jonas. I wish that he has a better memory. He is a forty-years-old man, and his memory is worst than it used to be. He can not remember details about the past, and its annoying. To illustrate, I'll describe an incident in our lives. Last month him and me had a huge argument about our wedding. Him and his brother wanted to wear jeans to the wedding, but I disagreed with theirs plans. Today, Jonas claims that the argument didn't happened and he had never mention jeans. I wish I recorded the conversation last month. Perhaps by the time we get married, we will forget the argument.

EXERCISE 5 "HOW" QUESTIONS

Complete each of the following questions by adding one of the missing words below:

far long many much often old

EXAMPLE: How much is that coat? Is it $15?

1. How ______________ is Jamie? Is she twenty years old?

2. How ______________ do you visit a doctor? Do you go twice a year?

3. How ______________ is the movie: two or three hours?

4. How ______________ people are in the lineup? Are there a lot of people?

5. How ______________ is Winnipeg? Is it more than 200 kilometres from here?

6. How ______________ was Tania when she moved away? Was she sixteen years old?

7. How ______________ have you been in college? Have you been here for one or two years?

8. How ______________ is that house? Does it cost more than $300,000?

9. How ______________ do you travel: once or twice a year?

EXERCISE 6 QUESTIONS

Students wrote questions about the article "Memories of 9/11" on page 12 of *Avenues 3: English Skills*. Identify and correct the errors in each of the following sentences.

EXAMPLE: Where ^does Brian Clark live?

1. When he started to work at the World Trade Center?

2. Why his colleagues were afraid?

3. How much long did Clark stay inside the burning building?

4. Since 2001, how many times did Clark visited New York?

5. Where he is living now?

6. What he did when the plane hit the building?

7. How long time did Stanley Praimnath spend under the desk?

8. In the future, what will be the reaction to a terrorist attack?

EXERCISE 7 FIVE KEY RULES

In this exercise, errors represent some major grammar problems. Errors are indicated in bold. Correct each error, then write a rule for each correction.

1. Everyone **have** problems. For example, my friend **want** a better job.

   Rule: ____

   ____

   See Unit 1 for more information about subject-verb agreement.

2. Since Dylan graduated, he **work** in advertising. He **made** many anti-drug commercials. He says that **he never took** drugs in his life.

   Rule: ____

   ____

   See Unit 3 for more information about present perfect tenses.

3. Children can learn languages more **easier** than adults can. Their brains can absorb new information **quicker** than adult brains can.

Rule: ____

____

See Unit 5 for more information about adverbs.

4. Mira and Samuel have **specifics** concerns about **theirs** ten-**years**-old son David.

Rule: ____

____

See Unit 5, page 53, for more information about adjectives and Unit 8, page 77, for more information about plurals.

5. When the plane hit the building, Brian Clark should **of** left immediately.

His colleagues should **of** gone downstairs instead of upstairs.

Rule: ____

____

See Unit 6 for more information about modal forms.

6. Last May, my grandfather died. If I **would have** known that he was ill, I would have spent more time with him.

Rule: ____

____

See Unit 7 for more information about conditional sentences.

7. People love to travel, **it's** a passion for them. They travel to practise using new languages, they also learn about different ways of thinking.

Rule: ____

____

See Unit 10 for more information about combining sentences.

8. Jan Wong said; "May God forgive me; I don't think they every will**." (124)**

Rule: ____

____

See Unit 11 for more information about punctuation.

Irregular Verb List

The following list has three columns:

- The **base form** appears in dictionaries. Use the base form in the present tense after auxiliaries such as *do*, *did*, *does*, *can*, and *should*, and after *to* in infinitives.

  EXAMPLE: You didn't help.

- Use the **simple past** form with the simple past tense.

  EXAMPLE: We bought a ticket yesterday.

- Use the **past participle** form in perfect and passive structures.

  EXAMPLE: She has been to England three times.

BASE FORM	SIMPLE PAST	PAST PARTICIPLE	BASE FORM	SIMPLE PAST	PAST PARTICIPLE
be	was/were	been	**do**	did	done
beat	beat	beat/beaten	**draw**	drew	drawn
become	became	become	**drink**	drank	drunk
begin	began	begun	**drive**	drove	driven
bend	bent	bent	**eat**	ate	eaten
bet	bet	bet	**fall**	fell	fallen
bind	bound	bound	**feed**	fed	fed
bite	bit	bitten	**feel**	felt	felt
bleed	bled	bled	**fight**	fought	fought
blow	blew	blown	**find**	found	found
break	broke	broken	**fit**	fit	fit
breed	bred	bred	**flee**	fled	fled
bring	brought	brought	**fly**	flew	flown
build	built	built	**forbid**	forbade	forbidden
burst	burst	burst	**foresee**	foresaw	foreseen
buy	bought	bought	**forget**	forgot	forgotten
catch	caught	caught	**forgive**	forgave	forgiven
choose	chose	chosen	**freeze**	froze	frozen
cling	clung	clung	**get**	got	got/gotten
come	came	come	**give**	gave	given
cost	cost	cost	**go**	went	gone
creep	crept	crept	**grind**	ground	ground
cut	cut	cut	**grow**	grew	grown
deal	dealt	dealt	**hang**[1]	hung	hung
dig	dug	dug	**have**	had	had

1. When *hang* means "to suspend by a rope, as in a form of capital punishment," then it is a **regular verb**. The past forms are *hanged*.

→

BASE FORM	SIMPLE PAST	PAST PARTICIPLE
hear	heard	heard
hide	hid	hidden
hit	hit	hit
hold	held	held
hurt	hurt	hurt
keep	kept	kept
kneel	knelt/kneeled	knelt/kneeled
know	knew	known
lay	laid	laid
lead	led	led
leave	left	left
lend	lent	lent
let	let	let
lie[2]	lay	lain
light	lit	lit
lose	lost	lost
make	made	made
mean	meant	meant
meet	met	met
mislead	misled	misled
mistake	mistook	mistaken
pay	paid	paid
prove	proved	proved/proven
put	put	put
quit	quit	quit
read[3]	read	read
ride	rode	ridden
ring	rang	rung
rise	rose	risen
run	ran	run
say	said	said
see	saw	seen
sell	sold	sold
send	sent	sent
set	set	set
shake	shook	shaken
shoot	shot	shot
show	showed	shown

BASE FORM	SIMPLE PAST	PAST PARTICIPLE
shrink	shrank	shrunk
shut	shut	shut
sing	sang	sung
sink	sank	sunk
sit	sat	sat
sleep	slept	slept
slide	slid	slid
speak	spoke	spoken
speed	sped	sped
spend	spent	spent
spin	spun	spun
split	split	split
spread	spread	spread
stand	stood	stood
steal	stole	stolen
stick	stuck	stuck
sting	stung	stung
stink	stank	stunk
strike	struck	struck
strive	strove	striven
swear	swore	sworn
sweep	swept	swept
swim	swam	swum
swing	swung	swung
take	took	taken
teach	taught	taught
tear	tore	torn
tell	told	told
think	thought	thought
throw	threw	thrown
thrust	thrust	thrust
understand	understood	understood
upset	upset	upset
wake	woke	woken
wear	wore	worn
win	won	won
withdraw	withdrew	withdrawn
write	wrote	written

2. *Lie* means "to rest or lie down, such as on a sofa or bed." When *lie* means "to tell a false statement," it is a regular verb: *lie–lied–lied*.
3. The present form of *read* is pronounced "reed." The simple past and past participle forms are pronounced "red."

Parts of Speech

PART OF SPEECH	DEFINITION	EXAMPLES
adjective	Adds information about the noun.	small, hot, beautiful, green
adverb	Adds information about the verb. Expresses time, place, or frequency.	easily, nicely, quickly, quietly sometimes, usually, often, never
conjunction	Connects two parts of a sentence. • **coordinating:** Connects two ideas of equal importance. • **subordinating:** Connects a subordinate (or secondary) idea to the main idea.	 and, but, so, or after, although, because, unless
determiner	Identifies or determines if the noun is specific or general.	a, an, the, this, that, these, those, each, every, much, many, some
noun (common)	Person, place or thing.	**Singular:** woman, cat, person **Plural:** women, cats, people
noun (proper)	Specific person, place or thing. Proper nouns are capitalized.	Jamaica, Doctor Reed, Samson, Lake Ontario, Golden Gate Bridge, Calgary
preposition	Shows a relationship between words (source, direction, location, etc.).	above, at, behind, below, for, from, of, to
pronoun	Replaces the noun.	he, she, it, us, ours, themselves
verb	Expresses an action or state.	talk, walk, think, drive

PRACTICE

Label each word with one of the following terms.

adjective, adverb, conjunction, determiner, noun (common), noun (proper), pronoun, preposition, verb

EXAMPLE: clear ___Adjective___

1. herself ____________

2. and ____________

3. human ____________

4. develop ____________

5. under ____________

6. blue ____________

7. often ____________

8. into ____________

9. theirs ____________

10. break ____________

11. children ____________

12. easily ____________

13. the ____________

14. Mrs. Grey ____________

Combining Ideas in Sentences

MAKING COMPOUND SENTENCES

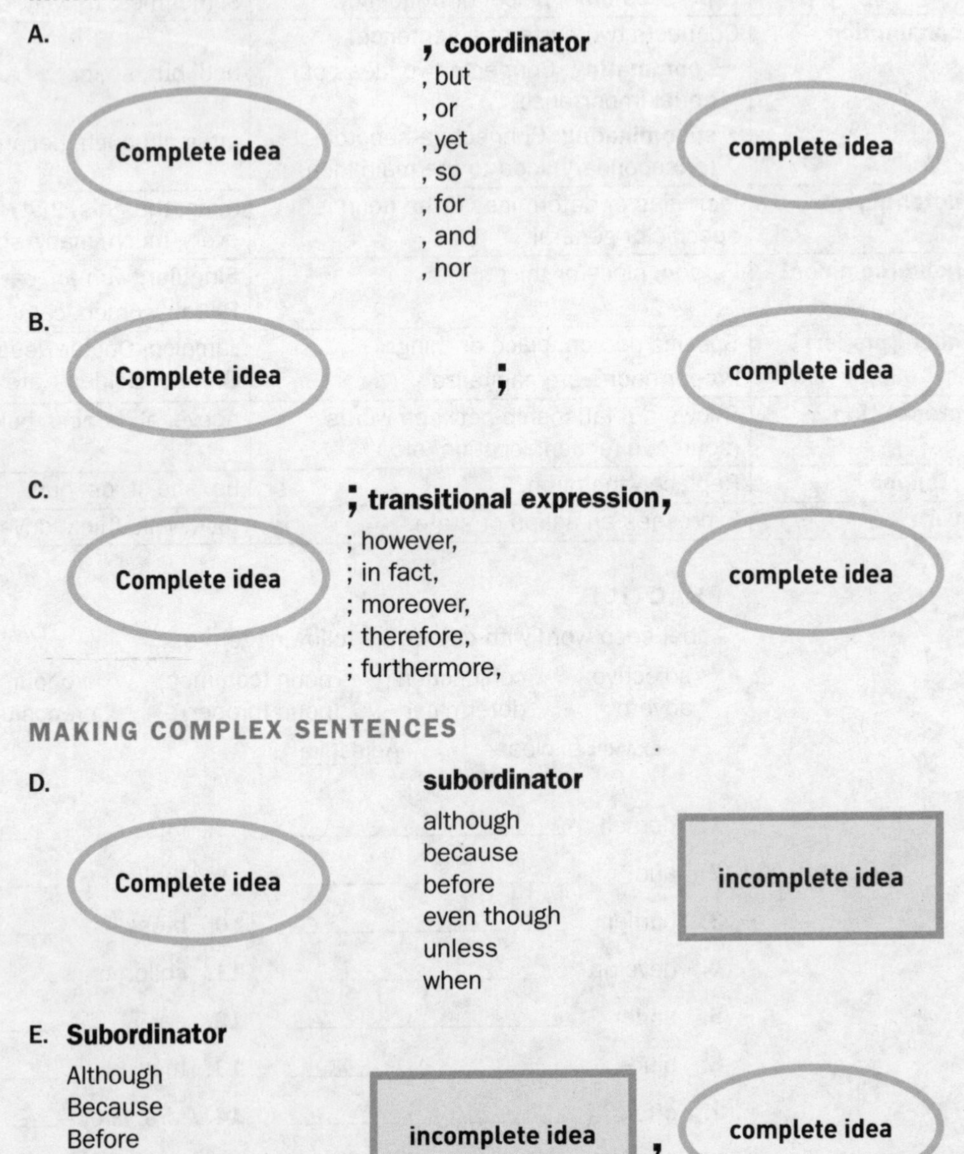

Spelling and Grammar Logs

In the first few pages of your writing portfolio or copybook, try keeping two logs to help you avoid repeating errors and to improve your writing.

SPELLING LOG

The goal of keeping a spelling log is to stop repeating errors. Every time you misspell a word, record both the mistake and the correction in your spelling log. Then, before you hand in a writing assignment, consult your list of misspelled words to ensure you're not repeating past errors.

Incorrect	Correct
finaly	finally
responsable	responsible

GRAMMAR LOG

The goal of keeping a grammar log is to stop repeating errors in sentence structure, mechanics, and punctuation. Each time a writing assignment is returned to you, identify one or two repeated grammar errors and add them to your grammar log. Next, consult the grammar log before you hand in new writing assignments in order to avoid making the same errors. For each type of grammar error, you could do the following:

1. Identify the assignment and write down the type of error.
2. In your own words, write a rule about the error.
3. Include an example from your writing assignment.

    1. Descriptive paragraph (Mar. 10) Fragment
    2. Sentences must have a subject and verb and express a complete thought.
    3. Also, my fears. ~~They~~ were irrational.

Spelling Log

Grammar Log

INDEX

PHOTO CREDITS

ALAMY
p. 9 © MARKA; p. 12 bottom, left © J. Sutton-Hibbert; p. 19 © Trinity Mirror/Mirropix; p. 30 © Pictorial Press Ltd.; p. 69 © Mandoga Media; pp. 70, 83 © ZUMA Wire Service; p. 82 © EIGHTFISH; p. 112 © EPA; p. 113 © arindambanerjee; p. 114 © Monkey Business Images; p. 124 © J. Sutton-Hibbert.

GAETZ, LYNNE: pp. 117, 129 top.

ISTOCKPHOTO: p. 18 © P. Wei; p. 32 © J. Bryson.

NATIONAL TRAFFIC SAFETY BOARD, USA: p. 40.

SHUTTERSTOCK
pp. 1 top, 10 top, 61 © S. Anna; p. 1 bottom © L. Smokovski; p. 3 © E. Durov; p. 4 © mmarcol; p. 5 © kaczor58; p. 7 top: © GlobetrotterJ; bottom: © irabel8; pp. 8, 105 © lynea; p. 10 bottom © Scenic Shutterbug; p. 11 © topten22photo; pp. 12 top, 24 © ifong; p. 12 bottom, right © Pinkcandy; p. 16 © holbox; p. 17 © B. Werkmann; p. 21 top: © Lisa S.; bottom: © J. Sharp; p. 22 © N. Tsvetkov; p. 24 bottom © ssguy; p. 25 © C. E. Santa-Maria; pp. 26 top, 36 top © T. Irina; pp. 26 middle, 57 middle, 109 © a. m. piacquadio; p. 28 © Contessa; p. 29 top: © A. Bayda; bottom: © nito; p. 31 © p. Michalis; p. 33 © elena1110; p. 34 bottom © D. Howell; p. 35 © beemanja; p. 36 bottom © H. Esteb; p. 37 © catwalker; pp. 38 top, 44 top © B. Rolff; p. 38 middle © K. R. Solana; p. 41 © L. Vandoorne; p. 42 © Seet; p. 43 © Blend Images; p. 44 bottom © Pius Lee; pp. 46 top, 55 top © A. Nekrassov; p. 48 © A. Muzika; p. 49 © I. Andriyanov; p. 50 © S. Duda; p. 51 © discpicture; p. 52 © D. Heinemann; p. 53 © t. sayig; p. 54 © Blueminiu; p. 55 middle © W. Muenzker; p. 56 © thieury; pp. 57 top, 64 top and bottom © U. Zunic; p. 59 top: © D. Sabljack; bottom: © JeniFoto; p. 60 © mtkang; p. 62 © J. Kershner; p. 63 © wavebreakmedia; p. 65 © A. Raths; pp. 66 top, 74 middle © italianestro; p. 66 middle © D. Beeler; p. 67 © photobank ch; p. 68 top: © Dhoxax; bottom: © Kom; p. 71 © D. Flowers; p. 72 © J. Wendler; p. 73 © haak78; p. 74 middle © dutourdumonde; p. 75 © bloomua; pp. 76 top, 88 top © A. Prado Photo; p. 76 middle © N. Vishneveckiy; p. 80 © sgm; p. 81 © pcruciatti; p. 84 © Citylights; p. 86 © C. Harvey; pp. 87, 139 © F. Mizioznikov; p. 88 bottom © arindambanerjee; p. 89 © Padmayogini; pp. 90 top, 100 top, 106 © Lightspring; p. 90 bottom © C. Brutiag; p. 92 © M. Gobson; p. 93 © Dariush M.; p. 94 © justasc; p. 96 © Elnur; p. 97 © V.P; p. 98 © kathmanduphotog; p. 100 middle © Tracing Tea; pp. 102 top, 115 top © S. Tucker; p. 102 middle © R. Bayer; p. 107 © Elsayyed; p. 110 © Pixachi; p. 111 © V. Smirnov; p. 116 © L. Martin; p. 117 bottom © g. yim; p. 120 © M. Blinkov; p. 121 © A. castelli; p. 123 © Nyuuness; p. 125 © bogdanhoda; p. 127 © silver-john; p. 128 © Danicak; p. 129 bottom © Neftali; p. 130 © V. Wrangel; pp. 131 top, 141 top © Djsash; p. 131 bottom © J. Krcmar; p. 134 © dream designs; p. 135 © Lisa B.; p. 137 © F. Gregory; p. 138 © Shutterwolf; p. 140 © V. Trofer; p. 142 © Ossile.

THINKSTOCK: p. 31.